D0429415

LIVING LIFE ON PURPOSE

Also by Greg Anderson

The 22 Non-Negotiable Laws of Wellness
The Cancer Conqueror
The Triumphant Patient
50 Essential Things to Do When the Doctor Says It's Cancer
Healing Wisdom

LIVING LIFE
ON PURPOSE

A Guide to Creating
a Life of Success
and Significance

Greg Anderson

HarperSanFrancisco
An Imprint of HarperCollins*Publishers*

LIVING LIFE ON PURPOSE: *A Guide to Creating a Life of Success and Significance.* Copyright © 1997 by Greg Anderson. All rights reserved. Printed in the United States of America. No part of this book may be used or reproduced in any manner whatsoever without written permission except in the case of brief quotations embodied in critical articles and reviews. For information address HarperCollins Publishers, 10 East 53rd Street, New York, NY 10022.

HarperCollins Web Site: http://www.harpercollins.com
HarperCollins®, ☷ ®, and HarperSanFrancisco™ are trademarks of HarperCollins Publishers, Inc.
FIRST EDITION

Library of Congress Cataloging-in-Publication Data

Anderson, Greg
    Living life on purpose : a guide to creating a life of success and significance / Greg Anderson. —1st ed.
ISBN 0–06–060196–5(cloth)
ISBN 0–06–060232–5(pbk.)
ISBN 0–06–060179–5(Int'l)
1. Self-actualization (Psychology) 2. Success—Psychological aspects.
3. Vocational guidance—Psychological aspects. I. Title.
BF637.S4A6 1997
158'.1—dc20   96–32302

97 98 99 00 01 RRD(H) 10 9 8 7 6 5 4 3 2 1

*To my wife Linda
and our daughter Erica.*

*You keep me
on purpose.*

CONTENTS

ACKNOWLEDGMENTS

My sincere gratitude is extended to the readers of my previous books. *Living Life on Purpose* came into being as a direct result of your interest and encouragement.

The collaboration of my Harper San Francisco editor, Caroline Pincus, made this effort possible. Thank you. To Tom Grady, my appreciation for catching the vision of this work and for sharing it with your entire team of exceptional coworkers.

To Linda and Erica, my deepest gratitude: you have supported my commitment to bring the message of total wellness to this world and given me the freedom to pursue my mission. Thank you.

Most of all, thank you God, for the magical gift of life and for the high privilege of this mission.

Life is too short to waste
In critic peep or cynic bark;
Quarrel or reprimand:
'Twill soon be dark;
Up! mind thine own aim, and
God speed the mark!

—_Ralph Waldo Emerson_

INTRODUCTION

Moments of happiness! They're pretty rare, aren't they?

Feeling that our life is significant! Seldom experienced by many people.

Personal peace! Mighty elusive for most of us.

"Call the VIP lounge," said the flight attendant. "Tell them they can bring her down any time."

I was on a plane preparing to leave Charleston, South Carolina; as is my custom, I had boarded early and was comfortably settled in my front-row window seat. For the past fifteen minutes, the remainder of the passengers had been filing on board and taking their assigned seats. With virtually everybody settled, I thought that we were just moments from shutting the door and leaving the gate.

But then came those words from the steward.

Within a couple of minutes, I heard the flight attendants, gathered around the front door, saying, "Here she comes." And indeed, through the doorway and around the corner came one of America's best-known and most beautiful supermodels.

She was gorgeous. Even with those eyes hidden behind sunglasses, you knew immediately who she was. Just a few minutes ago, I had been browsing through the magazine rack in the airport gift shop; her face had been on at least two different magazine covers. Over the years, she has graced the front cover of virtually every popular woman's magazine. Her television ads and appearances have made her recognizable to most of America. *People* magazine has repeatedly placed her on their "Twenty-five Most Beautiful People" list. She exudes a star quality that many Americans envy.

By the world's standards, this model and actress had it all. Fame—she was more famous and more revered than most television stars, movie personalities, sports figures, or national politicians. To the young women of America, she was perhaps the best known of the supermodels. If you judge success by fame, she was certainly successful.

Power—she was also powerful. My wife later shared with me a magazine article that told of a contract dispute between the supermodel and her agency. Her earning power was so important to the agency that she was able to break her existing contract and negotiate a new agreement. She could even pick her assignments, something few in the world of modeling can do. If you judge success by power, she was certainly successful.

Fortune—the same magazine article went on to say that in the previous year, her estimated earnings had exceeded ten million dollars. If success is judged by wealth, she was well on her way to being successful.

Fame, power, and fortune—all this added to her physical beauty. If ever anyone had the means to be happy, all the reasons to feel content and at peace with life, certainly she was the one.

And there she stood, ready to take her seat. The Charleston weather had been hot and humid that day. She was dressed accordingly: a tiny halter top, a pair of shorts, and sandals. They all matched perfectly and revealed much of this beautifully trim and fit body.

One of the flight attendants took her carry-on bag and pointed to the empty seat right beside me. "Make yourself at home," smiled the stewardess. "We'll be leaving momentarily."

I wanted to introduce myself. I wanted to talk. After all, how often does one get to spend some time with a supermodel? As she sat down and reached for her seat belt, I said, "Good afternoon. How are you doing today?"

Then it happened. What had been a pleasant smile on her face suddenly turned into an angry frown. What had been a confident, if somewhat nervous, persona turned into a boiling pot of anger. All my hopes for a pleasant conversation with a supermodel were shattered.

She snapped her seat-belt buckle in place and pulled the belt tight, then turned to me, and waving a perfectly manicured finger in my face, said in an exaggerated whisper, "Don't talk to me! Don't look at me! Don't bother me!"

With that she tugged at her seat belt one last time and turned in her seat so that as much of her back as possible faced me. She crossed one thin leg over the other, pulled a book out of her oversized purse, turned on the reading light, and retreated into her own world.

Not more than two hours earlier, I had been conducting an executive retreat for the partners of one of America's Big Six accounting firms. The subject had been "creating wellness," and our focus had been on bringing balance to our lives. We had put a considerable amount of time into understanding that the fulfilled life requires both success and significance—and that both of these qualities start within. The message: self-knowledge and self-control must precede effective dealings with the world at large.

I thought about this message and contrasted it with the behavior of the woman sitting next to me. Her fame, power, and fortune would be the envy of ninety-nine out of a hundred people on the planet. But you did not have to be a genius to recognize immediately that she was a very unhappy person.

Where do you go to find happiness?

To fame? Recognition by the public ebbs and flows. It is not permanent. Happiness cannot be found in fame.

To power? Control over one's own destiny, or the destiny of others, does not ensure happiness or contentment, and it certainly does not promise significance.

To fortune? We all know wealthy people and can see that they have just as many problems as you and I do. In fact, wealth brings more problems. Often people who have large sums of money are less happy, more lonely, and more suspicious of other people's motives. Fortune doesn't ensure happiness or significance.

How, then, do you find the happiness, the significance, the sense of personal peace that make for the great life?

This is a book about the life-transforming power of living one's life "on purpose"—of living out one's life mission.

In this book, you will meet people who *have* lived their lives on purpose. You'll also be introduced to a formula that will help you discover and live out your mission. And you'll be inspired to commit to responding positively and daily to the call of mission and higher purpose.

This book will change your life—if you let it.

If you will allow the life-mission formula to lead you, a whole new and higher level of living will become available to you. What is this formula? It is a simple but far from simplistic outline of how to identify the purpose that you have been given. The formula is:

VISION + SERVICE × PASSION = MISSION

Wherever you are right now—winning or losing, succeeding or failing, feeling enthusiastic or depressed, happy or sad, you can deepen the significance and heighten the success of your life if you will put this formula to work for you.

Vision—Capturing a sense of what might be.

Service—Giving of oneself to others.

Passion—Having a love affair with your life.

Mission—Living out the reason you were put here on earth at this moment in history.

It's time for all of us, as nations and as individuals, to throw off the weights of apathy and pessimism that have so permeated the past two generations. In a world filled with mediocrity, greed, even death and destruction, it is time to recognize that we face a major turning point and that we have a choice. We can choose to follow our life mission.

It's time, in both our personal and corporate histories, to reach for a new vision, where some fundamental redefinitions are required, and where our table of values can be reviewed.

It's time we each seek our own mission—the unique reason we are here and the unique contributions that we are to make. This is a moment when we must reach for a state of life and well-being measured not simply in terms of income, or status, or power, or recognition but in terms of significance, service, and joy.

The fact is that as difficult, frustrating, and fearful as these times are, they are also fascinating. This is because you and I have a pivotal role to play in attaining the larger planetary objectives of peace and prosperity. For these objectives will be achieved only when each of us as individuals and each of our organizations defines and lives out our true mission.

Following the formula, VISION + SERVICE × PASSION = MISSION, starts us along this path. Now we know! The secret is out! Apply this formula. Enjoy the results. And you, too, will lead a life of success and significance.

1

VISION

I have a dream . . .

Martin Luther King, Jr.

. . .

VISION + SERVICE × PASSION = MISSION

■ ■ ■

"Who am I?"

This eternal question is one of the most difficult yet most pragmatic inquiries that any person can make.

Grasping a keen inner sense of who we are, of where our abilities and interests lie, and of what our prospects are for living a full and satisfying life is fundamental to attaining success. It is also a requirement for achieving a life of significance.

Asking the "Who am I?" question is simultaneously frightening and empowering. As proof, I have only to look at an incredible personal experience I had some dozen years ago.

In 1984, I was diagnosed with metastatic lung cancer. A surgeon told me I had thirty days to live.

In an effort to understand what others had done to live through "terminal" medical diagnoses, I began a series of interviews. In three and a half years, I talked to over 550 "survivors" of terminal diagnoses.

There were many themes that came through in this study. But none was as important as the decision to live out one's life mission—to "dance my dance," as one breast cancer survivor emphatically put it.

In my book 50 *Essential Things to Do When the Doctor Says It's Cancer,* I asked readers to respond to a survey on cancer and recovery. Over and over, with sincerity and certainty, reader after reader claimed that recovery is linked to having a reason to live. Over the years, some eleven thousand readers have responded to that survey. Fully 72 percent of the respondents link recovery, in part, to understanding and living out important purposes in their lives.

The survey respondents include CEOs, members of Congress, public service administrators, military officers, the unemployed, the retired, the young, the old, males, and females.

Respondent after respondent has talked about getting well after making a deep decision to follow his or her particular purpose in life—to live out a mission. These respondents seemed to rediscover their spiritual heartbeat. When their mission became real, life followed.

A housewife wrote, "The reason I survived is that I must stay alive in order to help my grandchildren. I may have failed my daughter, but I will not fail my granddaughters."

A state legislator wrote, "Illness was my wake-up call. I have so many goals yet to accomplish. This state needs me. I decided I needed to get on with the tasks at hand, ill or not."

A successful real estate developer replied, "When I turned my efforts toward bringing a chapter of Habitat for Humanity to our region, my illness simply fell away. I've found my calling."

IDENTIFYING THE FIRST REQUIREMENT

The critical factor in achieving success and significance? No doubt it's a sense of mission—and mission begins with a vision of who we are and what we can become.

Richard Hayward found his vision. A Native American of the Mashantucket Pequots, Hayward was elected tribal chairman in 1975. "A common practice among my tribal ancestors was to send young men into the wilderness on a vigil or a vision quest. The purpose of this vigil was to assist the young warrior in finding his vision, his spirit guide, and his purpose."

Hayward had a vision of who he was and what he could become. The Mashantucket Pequots were not officially recognized by Congress at the time Hayward was elected. The tribe did not have all the official rights and privileges Congress grants to American Indians. Hayward sought to change that.

In 1983, Hayward won federal recognition. His vision was to create peace and prosperity for the members of his tribe.

While some have criticized Hayward's strategy, he is proud to point out that his Fox Woods Resort Casino in Ledyard, Connecticut, now contributes an average annual stipend of two hundred thousand dollars per adult tribe member. In fact, the Mashantuckets were able to give ten million dollars to the Smithsonian Institution's new Native American Museum. And Hayward is now urging the tribe to open its own museum.

Vision—
a sense of
who we are
and
what we can
become—
is the
first requirement
for mission.

"Who am I?" Hayward asked. Part of his answer was that he was a person of significance. He saw himself as someone who could make a difference.

That's vision—possessing a sense of who we are and what we can become—and it's the first requirement for mission. Vision creates focus, an agenda, an unparalleled concern with the outcome of one's life. Find your vision, and life changes.

As we begin our process of discovery, we need a working definition of what a life mission is and what it is not. A life mission is a continuing responsibility that one is specifically fit to fulfill. Your mission is a calling, a lifework, a vocation. It is not a job, a role, or a goal that we can check off a list after we have accomplished it.

One's mission is something more, something far greater. It is a way of living and being—on a deeper, more significant level—that results in actions that change lives. Part of your discovery process will involve exploring these deeper dimensions of your own life mission.

ACKNOWLEDGING MISSION AS BIRTHRIGHT

You were born to greatness. Having a life mission implies that the world has need of you. In fact, the world has been preparing you to fill this need with one incredible life experience after another. Finding and fulfilling your potential will lead to your highest experience in this life. Believe it, you have a mission. It is the gateway to your personal greatness.

*You were
born to
greatness.*

*The world
has need
of you.*

It may seem difficult for you to believe that the world has need of you. It does. It not only needs you, but also needs the *best* of you, the finest you have to offer. And the world needs this finest offering at the specific place and for the specific purposes where it will make a crucial difference in other people's lives.

Les Brown is living proof that you can live your mission by giving of your best self. He came up the hard way; born in poverty, adopted and raised by a single mother, he was labeled "educable mentally retarded" as a youth. Convinced by a teacher that he was capable of contributing to the world, Les, with no formal education after high school, became a disc jockey, a community activist, and served three terms in the Ohio state legislature. He then went on to become one of this country's preeminent public speakers, a television talk-show host, and the husband of entertainer Gladys Knight.

Believe it. No matter where we start, the world has need of us at our best.

It may also seem difficult to believe that you were born to greatness. You were. You have the ability to develop majesty of character. You have the capacity for self-love. And you can serve with love, the highest sign of greatness.

Thomas Merton captured the essence of being born to greatness when he wrote about self-love:

> What do I mean by loving ourselves properly? I mean first of all, desiring to live, accepting life as a very great gift, and a great good, not because of what it gives us, but because of what it enables us to give others.

Yes, self-love is central to our vision for mission.

A vision for mission is something that is compelling and that pulls you toward your mission. The vision inspires a degree of intensity that, coupled with commitment, is magnetic. A vision for mission can mobilize people and resources in the service of higher purposes.

Meals on Wheels is an example of a powerful vision at work. "I was determined to get involved on a grassroots level," said Anise Yarbrough, an Albuquerque, New Mexico, homemaker and freelance writer. "I just don't see that politicians get a lot done; few ever really change anything. So I volunteer for Meals on Wheels, delivering dinners to shut-ins and the elderly."

Vision grabs. First it grabs the imagination of the leader. Then it commands the attention of others and helps people get on the bandwagon.

Of course some politicians do get things done, both in and out of office. The former governor of Pennsylvania, George M. Leader, is a prime example. Observing the decline of the inner cities in his state, Leader set out to teach values to kids ages six to twelve. "You absolutely, positively must get to them in the formative years," he says.

Convinced that he needed incentives in order to get kids' attention, he put in place two programs that promised a free bicycle and a free computer to those who would work to earn them.

Sharing his vision with others, he focused their attention on the problems of kids lost to the street. An agenda emerged. People began to contribute used bicycles. Corporations donated used computers. Because his vision and intentions are compelling, they pull people toward the project. Governor Leader's personal intensity drives the entire effort. But it is his vision of making this world a better place that drives Leader himself.

Daniel Burrus noted that ordinary people were increasingly fumbling with cellular phones and computer keyboards. A former teacher, Burrus figured he could use his teaching skills to make these devices seem easy. From this simple vision was born Burrus Research Associates.

Burrus's undeviating attention is focused on corporate audiences who hate to read manuals on how to use and profit from the Internet, desktop video conferencing, and the like. Some would call Burrus obsessed. But it is his focused vision that drives his successful business.

Talk to most people who feel they are living out their mission and you'll see, again and again, people who are passionate about an idea. They possess a vision and are possessed by it. This intensity focuses their attention. And focusing one's attention is the first step toward implementing and orchestrating a vision for mission.

Yet this intensity must not be forced. Chef Wolfgang Puck was described by one of his restaurant managers as playful. "He reminds me of a child at play—very determined. He will say, like a child, 'Let's try this.' And we will. We make it fun!"

Vision includes balance. If the vision focuses only on one aspect of success—such as economic gain—it creates an imbalance.

One of my saddest experiences was to see a successful friend fall victim to a vision gone awry. He created a computer program that made a portion of his retail store's sales "disappear." He kept the difference—in cash. Today, he sits in federal prison, serving a four-and-a-half-year sentence.

Balance. Vision must encompass body, mind, and spirit, addressing wellness in the broadest sense. It must recognize that life is complete only when it is lived in balance, when it is driven by such master values as integrity, service, and love.

CHOOSING A FUTURE

When a vision is balanced, it animates. It inspires and transforms purpose into action.

Poet Maya Angelou uniquely demonstrates the balance required of vision. "I didn't know about making money from writing as a child. I thought success meant having an attaché case and a pair of shoes and bags that matched." Her best-known book, *I Know Why the Caged Bird Sings,* spent over three years on the *New York Times* best-seller list.

Says Angelou, "The first thing you do is . . . convince yourself that the undertaking in which you are involved is manifestly important and nearly impossible. That belief draws out the kind of drives that makes people strong, that puts you in pursuit intellectually." She is speaking of vision.

Vision concentrates one's attention on choosing a future and making it a reality.

This future is tied to our initial question, "Who am I?" For each of us to choose a direction, we must first have developed a mental image of a possible and desirable way of living in the future. This image, this vision, may be as vague as a dream or as precise as a specific goal. But a vision for mission must exist.

Famous health enthusiast Jack LaLanne studied premed in college, planning to become a medical doctor. He also took a chiropractic course. But he discovered he was more interested in helping people through prevention—before they became ill. "That became my mission—to help people find health and fitness."

This simple statement of vision focused LaLanne's energy. At twenty-one, LaLanne opened the nation's first health studio on the third floor of an old office building in Oakland, California. "I was forty years ahead of my time," he says. "But by then I knew more about the body than most doctors."

He focused on this mission. The vision had grabbed him.

LaLanne developed the first models of the exercise equipment that now is standard in health spas. He was the first to encourage women, invalids, and the elderly to exercise for health.

"It was the vision that led to my success. People thought I was a charlatan or a nut," LaLanne says. "The doctors were against me—they said working out with weights would give people heart attacks and they would lose their sex drive; women would look like men. Even the coaches predicted that athletes would get muscle-bound if they used weights."

LaLanne's vision sustained him. Today all world-class athletes work out with weights. "I understand the working of the body, the muscles, and bones, and nerves," he says. "What I was doing was scientifically correct, starting with a healthy diet—and today everybody knows it. It was that vision of what we can be that carried me through."

*Vision
concentrates
one's attention
on choosing a
future
and
making it
happen.*

Vision implies change. The person who would embrace his or her mission must understand that the vision for that mission offers a view of a realistic, credible, attractive future for himself or herself. The vision must point toward a condition that is better in some important ways than one's current state.

A vision, in other words, is a target that beckons.

Dave Thomas, founder and chairman of Wendy's International, had a vision to own a chain of restaurants. While he was working for the Hobby House chain in Fort Wayne, Indiana, his boss offered him the opportunity to realize his vision.

The deal was a risky one: Thomas would take over the management of four failing Kentucky Fried Chicken franchises in Columbus, Ohio. If he could revive the stores, pay off a deficit of two hundred thousand dollars, and turn a profit, he would get 45 percent ownership. Ignoring the advice of friends and even of Colonel Harlan Sanders, the Kentucky Fried Chicken founder, Thomas moved his family to Columbus.

He was driven by a vision of a future state that was preferable to his current one. Thomas quickly realized that the stores were failing because they carried too many items. He cut the menu down to just a few choices and bargained with the local radio station to trade chicken for radio ads.

The restaurants prospered. Thomas added four more locations in Columbus. In 1968, at age thirty-five, he sold the restaurants back to Kentucky Fried Chicken for one and a half million dollars, and he became regional operations director for KFC, traveling with the Colonel to oversee some three hundred restaurants.

The vision of a preferred future state guided Thomas further; he still wanted to run his own business. In 1969, he opened his first Wendy's Old-Fashioned Hamburgers in downtown Columbus. The menu featured fresh, made-to-order hamburgers, chili, french fries, soft drinks, and a Frosty dessert. He named it after his daughter, Melinda, nicknamed Wendy.

Vision grabs everyone it touches. The modest plans that Thomas started with—a small chain of restaurants in Columbus and a place for his five children to work in the summer—drew the interest of hundreds of people. The concept was a popular one, and the chain expanded.

A true vision takes on a life of its own. In 1973, twenty investors encouraged Thomas to begin franchising and selling franchises for entire cities and regions. More than one thousand units opened in the first hundred months. And by 1979, annual sales totaled one billion dollars. Today the chain, even though it has undergone some restructuring, is highly successful and profitable. It is not just a place that dispenses food but has also offered the opportunity for many people to experience their own economic freedom.

It all started with a vision that focused attention.

To understand why vision is essential to discovering one's mission, we need only reflect on why people seek a mission in the first place. Individuals embark on missions in the hope of receiving rewards. Depending on the individual involved, the rewards may be economic, or they may be primarily psychosocial benefits, such as status, self-esteem, a sense of accomplishment, or a meaningful existence.

When an individual has a clear sense of a desired future state, and when this image becomes the central guiding force in his or her life, then that person is able to make contributions that are typically rewarded. But it's the vision that we create—the vision that allows us to see ourselves as significant, as having competence—that is the all-important starting point. The result is the creation of a sense of significance that transforms mere human existence into highly inspired and motivating *raison d'être* that literally casts off obstacles in pursuit of mission.

MAKING A DIFFERENCE

"Have you been inhaling glue fumes too long?" asked one of Art Fry's coworkers. This attitude was just one of many obstacles that Art encountered in the early days of a quest that has become a huge success.

Art had a problem that he needed to solve. While singing in his church choir, he kept losing his place in the choir book because his bookmark slipped. When the bookmark disappeared, Art was left fumbling through the pages when it came time for the next song.

But Art Fry was no ordinary choir member. Having worked his way through the University of Minnesota by selling pots and pans door to door and possessing a naturally inquisitive nature, he had a knack for inventing things. After he earned a degree in chemical engineering, he landed a job as a product development specialist at 3M Corporation.

Art's inventiveness helped him come up with a bookmark that had a bit of stickum on it. His idea worked so well that

Art looked for other applications. He decided his sticky bookmark would make a great little memo pad.

The people at 3M could not connect with his vision. But Art had notepads made up and began giving them out. One day, when one of his bosses walked through a snowstorm for several blocks just to get more, Art knew his idea had great potential.

Indeed it did. Art Fry's solution to losing his place in the choir book resulted in the venerable 3M Post-Its notepads. Today, an entire product line is built around his invention. It earns his company millions of dollars each year. And Art has risen to a high-paying and esteemed position within 3M.

That's vision at work. When individuals feel that they can make a difference, can improve a situation for themselves or for the society in which they live, then it is much more likely that they will bring vigor, enthusiasm, and success to their tasks. This is the magical part of a vision for mission.

The business world is filled with real-life examples of people who caught a vision for mission and pursued it. Curtis L. Carlson, CEO and chairman of Carlson Companies of Minneapolis, Minnesota, started on his mission of serving the travel needs of America with trading stamps for grocery stores. A successful young soap salesman for Proctor and Gamble, Curt talked his landlord into supplying him with working capital by deferring a month's rent—which was then fifty-five dollars. Carlson invested the rent money in some printed books of trading stamps. His new business, the Gold Bond Stamp Company ("gold" for value, "bond" for safety), was born.

Carlson's vision of a preferred future state guided him. His first sale was a $14.50 order from a small grocery. "If this works," he told his wife, "thousands of stores all over America will be buying the Gold Bond Stamps."

Carlson's optimism carried him through. Today he is chief executive officer and chairman of Carlson Companies, the successor to the Gold Bond Stamp Company and the fifteenth largest privately held company in the nation. Among its more well-known subsidiaries are the Carlson Travel Group, operating as "Ask Mr. Foster" in the United States; the Radisson Hotel chain; and TGI Fridays, with 150 restaurants throughout the country.

Vision: it's the first requirement for mission.

Vision takes the form of enthusiasm, commitment, pride, and the willingness to work hard and go the extra mile. You can "feel" the energy that emanates from vision almost from the moment you meet somebody who possesses it. This person's focus on his or her vision mobilizes not just physical resources but emotional and spiritual assets as well. Vision brings to life values, commitment, and aspirations.

Vision makes people unstoppable; lack of vision can make the same people easily stoppable. Remember Buster Douglas, the unknown fighter who beat heavyweight champion Mike Tyson? Vision played an important part in the brief but brilliant career of Douglas.

In his fight with Tyson, Douglas was knocked down hard. Lying on the canvas, he was a man possessed by a vision; he had powerful motivation to get up.

At that point, Buster Douglas was being flattened by life. Some called him a "bum"; he had only recently been released from an alcohol recovery center; he was broke. His personal life was in disarray. His only hope was this fight.

Buster Douglas got up because he was determined to prove that he was not a bum. And not only did he get up but he won that fight because of the power of his vision.

Buster Douglas was crowned heavyweight champion of the world. Then he had to defend his title. His first—and last defense—was against Evander Holyfield. But the Buster Douglas who showed up for that match had a different vision. Since he was already champion, Douglas had a guaranteed payday of twenty-four million dollars even if he lost. A whole different vision was planted in his mind compared to his fight for survival in that first match with Tyson.

Visions lead. And Buster Douglas lost that second fight. The lesson: vision must grab us, vision must motivate us, for it is our vision for mission that drives us. It has to matter very deeply to us that this vision come to pass; otherwise, we may not have the strength of purpose to persevere.

THE DIFFERENCE BETWEEN A JOB AND A MISSION

Although "job" and "mission" are not synonymous, many people apply the principle of vision to work. Rightly so. Vision works at work. It is important to understand the difference between what a visionary can do and what a manager can do. The manager operates on the physical resources alone. The manager mobilizes capital, human skills, raw materials, and technology. A competent manager can make it possible for people to earn a living. An excellent manager is efficient at seeing that work is done productively, on schedule, and with quality.

But it remains for the visionary to instill pride, satisfaction, commitment, and enthusiasm in the work. It is the vision for mission that inspires people to greatness, triggering higher levels of achievement and contributing to meeting worthwhile ends. There is an emotional appeal in vision. It satisfies some of the most fundamental human needs—the need to be important, the need to make a difference, the need to feel useful, and the desire to leave a legacy.

With all the benefits that a sharply defined vision can inspire, it is surprising that every person does not take great care to develop a clear image of his or her desire for a future state. Instead, most people do not have a vision. Or the visions of many people are out of focus and lack coherence. For many others, the impediments to mission are overwhelming.

IMPEDIMENTS TO MISSION

I recently spoke with a leader of one of our Cancer Conquerors support groups, the organization I started following my "terminal" cancer diagnosis. She shared that she was no longer working on her dream to write a book. When I asked why, she said that by the time she had finished working sixty hours a week, she just didn't have the time or energy left to act on her goal.

She is not alone. Numerous studies conclude that Americans are working longer, enjoying it less, and fearing that they might lose their job any day. This is not living out a vision!

We often must fan the fire of our vision. Life does not always present us with the ideal situation in which to pursue our mission. Like it or not, there are forces in this world that make the attainment of our mission difficult. We could construct long lists of reasons why any particular vision for mission cannot be accomplished. But if we study those reasons, I believe we'll see that they fall into four categories:

1. *People*. There is no question that many people defer to others in articulating their vision and mission in life. A wife defers to societal expectations; a husband defers to his boss; a worker defers to a supervisor; a gang member defers to a gang leader; a person on welfare defers to a government program—the list is endless.

The reality is that there are people who will readily paint a vision for us if we allow them to. We need to ask ourselves whether we are "dancing our own dance" or responding to the music of others. A life lived according to another's vision, whether that vision comes from parent, spouse, friend, or institution, only rarely satisfies. Shakespeare's words put it well: "To thine own self be true."

2. *Pride*. How difficult it is for some people to say, "I was wrong." Or "I need help." Admitting our faults or weaknesses and our all-too-human nature is not easy. But it is essential. Pride can stand in the way of living out our vision.

A friend of mine had a drinking problem. But I was codependent—I didn't confront him. Finally one day, after a particularly disturbing encounter with him the previous night, I pumped up my courage and said, "Bill, you have to stop drinking until you drop. Let me help you." Bill exploded in angry denial. His pride was wounded. It was nearly two months before he would speak to me again.

Happiness comes, and vision is transformed, when we are able to admit we need help. We don't need to be afraid of embarrassment or rejection. What we do need to fear is what may happen when we are constantly denying our lack, covering up our needs, and attempting to hide our short-comings. This is called pride, and it is a mighty force that will surely impede our mission.

3. *Perfectionism.* For some people, good enough never is. When we feel that everything needs to be perfect, we limit our options. To focus on obtaining perfection in our mission is to fixate on end results. Our mission outcomes, in a real sense, are out of our hands. We have control only over the efforts we make. The results are in God's hands.

"I was always criticized by my father," shared an attendee at one of our week-long wellness programs. "My God, I could never please him. I suppose that's why I work too much today. It's an attempt to please him. If I work hard enough, maybe I can be perfect in his eyes."

Perfectionism, held as an ideal for ourselves or for others, is an excuse for us to settle for mission in words only. But mission requires action. Wait for the perfect time or for the perfect results and we will wait the rest of our lives. As management guru Tom Peters taught us: "Do it. Try it. Fix it." Action, not perfection.

4. *Pessimism.* Thoughts are things. They create energy. You receive exactly what you send out. Pessimism is a mental and verbal bombardment of negativity that will destroy your chances to find and accomplish your mission.

Pessimism has its false payoffs. I have worked with tens of thousands of people who are struggling with illness. Sickness can command attention; we call this a "secondary gain." In our family, we have a relative who, every time we're together, drags out all his physical problems. And what happens? He becomes the focus of attention. I see this repeated wherever I speak. Negativity can be very powerful.

Pessimism has another side. If you predict something will turn out "badly" and it does turn out that way, then you don't have to blame yourself for being wrong! Your assumption all along that the idea or project wouldn't work becomes, after all, the correct one. In addition, pessimism sounds so authoritative; it carries a sense of realism, wisdom, and clarity. It can seem so "mature."

But the fact is that optimism is a requirement for mission. You are aiming for one result: to remove any barriers, blocks, or obstacles that keep you from finding and working toward your life mission. Pessimism is the most significant impediment of all.

All these forces—people, pride, perfectionism, and pessimism—contribute to a massive assault that can keep us from living a mission-based life. They create great uncertainty and an abundance of conflicting images in our lives.

Sad examples of these powerful forces are everywhere. A former head of publishing giant Simon and Schuster was unable to stop himself from degrading and humiliating subordinates. He demonstrated all the impediments: other people were doing things wrong; pride in his own ideas was high; perfectionism was his trademark; and pessimism ruled his judgment. Another company eventually bought Simon and Schuster and fired the editor in chief in a very nasty public display. Explaining why the acquiring company had done so, a *New York Times Magazine* article said that the man "had not been a team player."

The *New York Times* reporter Roger Rosenblatt asked "if he [the former editor in chief] had been able to double Simon and Schuster's business, would you still have fired him?"

"Probably," replied the new CEO.

Look closely at this real-life situation. Every impediment to mission was at play: deficits in people skills, inappropriate pride, undue perfectionism, and overwrought pessimism. This editor in chief would have ranked low in what author Daniel Goleman calls "emotional intelligence," or "EQ." Goleman defines your EQ as the power not only to control emotions but also to perceive them. Failing to do so can be costly—perhaps even the greatest impediment to mission.

The answer: make vision for mission more imperative than ever. If we do not have a coherent vision of the future, these forces can conspire to shatter our mission at any time. Restoring a sense of purpose, a focus, is the only solution.

SEARCHING FOR SIGNIFICANCE

A vision for mission requires natural shifts in perception and behavior. Everyone can make these changes. We find that often the vision does not even need to be original. Rather, it has its seeds in the ordinary, even negative, experiences of our life.

Oprah Winfrey was born and grew up in rural Mississippi, where she was raised by her grandmother. Turning nine,

Oprah was sent to live with her mother in Milwaukee. It was a difficult life, and during the next five years she was repeatedly sexually abused.

Oprah recalls those years as a terrifying time in her life, where her fears and deep sense of guilt turned her into a rebellious and uncontrollable teenager. Eventually, as a last resort, she was sent to Nashville to live under her father's strict discipline.

"Daddy turned my life around by making me see that being your best was the best that you could be." Oprah worked side by side with him in his grocery store every day after school. Vernon Winfrey and his wife, Zelma, Oprah's stepmother, were determined to teach her the importance of discipline and education, so they required Oprah to read a book every week and write a book report on it. This discipline was just what she needed.

Oprah finished high school and went on to graduate from Tennessee State University. She majored in speech communications. At nineteen, still a college student, she became the youngest news anchor and the first African-American woman ever to work at WTVF-TV in Nashville.

Oprah was recruited by the executives of WJZ-TV in Baltimore, and in 1976 she joined the staff as coanchor of the *Six O'clock News*. But Baltimore was where she discovered her talent for conversational television. She became the city's most popular TV personality as cohost of *People Are Talking*.

"I had a vision I could succeed," said Oprah, sharing her philosophy with students. "You have to believe that you can succeed, believe that you can be whatever your heart desires, and be willing to work for it."

*Vision
for mission
requires
natural shifts in
perception
and
behavior.*

Seven years later, Oprah's vision led her to Chicago to become host of *AM Chicago*. The show quickly became first in its time period, and in less than a year it was expanded to an hour and renamed *The Oprah Winfrey Show*. Four years later, Oprah purchased her show from Capital Cities/ABC and assumed full ownership and production responsibilities.

The show was syndicated and immediately became the number-one daytime talk show in the United States. It remains that today. The broadcast is seen in twenty-four countries by fourteen million viewers each day. Says Oprah, "I believe my show has been successful because my vision is always to create a format that informs, encourages, and enlightens, as well as entertains. My intent is never to exploit."

Vision—the word itself brings to mind grand schemes, great dreams, and global issues. But vision is not reserved just for the elite; it is available to all. And the best visions for mission come directly out of our everyday experiences of life.

CONSTRUCTING A VISION: PAST, PRESENT, FUTURE

People who construct great visions, whether they are janitors or parents or chief executives or senators, are great askers. They pay attention to the responses that life constantly gives them.

Growing up in the black ghetto of Baltimore, young Thurgood Marshall was an early, though unwilling, student of the U.S. Constitution.

Often in mischief, he was required to stay after school as punishment for his classroom antics. For each infraction of a rule, Marshall was required to memorize a portion of the Constitution. As a result, Marshall reported, he soon knew the whole thing by heart.

Marshall's primary school teachers would have been astonished if they could have foreseen that their unruly pupil would one day put that knowledge into practice as a distinguished attorney and then as this nation's first African-American United States Supreme Court Justice.

Thurgood Marshall found his vision from his past, his present, and various alternative images of future possibilities. We can find our vision in the same manner.

The Past

Born in Baltimore, Marshall was named after his grandfather, a proprietor of a local grocery store. In a real sense his grandfather was a model and a mentor. Marshall often looked to the past for analogies and precedents from his grandfather's life that he might apply to new situations.

Marshall did well in high school and enrolled in Lincoln University, which was known as the "black Princeton." During the summers, Marshall worked as a baker, a bellhop, and a dining-car waiter. He was constantly talking to a wide variety of his colleagues in those organizations, building a mental model of what worked and what didn't work.

Marshall looked to the past and projected what would happen to him and his entire race if it continued on the same course. The past was enormously powerful in pushing Marshall toward a career as an attorney. Prevented by the "Jim Crow" laws from entering law school at the University of Maryland in his hometown, he decided on Howard University Law School in Washington, D.C. His law school experience confirmed that America needed to be awakened in order to rise above racial injustice. The past formed the vision on which he built his life.

The Present

Thurgood Marshall was hired as counsel to the Baltimore NAACP. Through this work he saw the early warning signs of impending change. In fact, the present gives all of us the opportunity to create a laboratory in which we can experiment with our new vision. This is what Thurgood Marshall did.

In 1936, Marshall mounted his first successful civil rights case, *Murray vs. Maryland,* which upheld the right of black students to attend the University of Maryland Law School—from which he had once been barred.

From this experience, Marshall went on to become chief legal officer of the NAACP. The present offered him an ongoing opportunity to battle for minority rights, and he was involved in most of the major civil rights cases of the fifties and sixties. He argued thirty-two cases before the United States Supreme Court, winning twenty-nine and earning the title of "Mr. Civil Rights."

The Future

Our vision needs to focus on and address the future. To ensure that it does, we need to study the conditions that may prevail in the future.

Thurgood Marshall was an expert at studying the long-term trends, particularly in race relations. President Kennedy and President Johnson both nominated Marshall to posts, including the Second Circuit Court of Appeals in 1961 and solicitor general of the United States in 1965. In 1967, Marshall succeeded Justice Tom Clark on the Supreme Court bench.

From these vantage points Marshall gained a clear vision of where the civil rights struggle needed to go. As he peered into the future, he expanded his vision. He reflected, "I submit that the history of black America demonstrates the importance of getting rid of hostile laws and seeking the security of new friendly laws.

"Provided there is a determination to enforce it, law can change things for the better," he said at a White House conference on civil rights. "There is very little truth in the old refrain that one cannot legislate equality."

This was Thurgood Marshall's vision of the future. He looked for structural clues, such as the laws of the time. We can develop a scenario of what the future may look like if certain structural changes are made. And we can examine the implications of each scenario for ourselves and for the vision we hold.

Some say you cannot predict the future. But the truth is that we can be inundated with information about the future. Only a small part of this information may prove useful, however, and we need to analyze it carefully in order to recognize the signposts that will help us develop our vision. It is in the interpretation of these visions of the future that the real art of living a mission-based life lies.

Just as the historian attempts to take information about the past and construct an interpretation of the forces that may have been at work, so we select, organize, structure, and interpret information about the future in an effort to construct a viable vision.

But we have one distinct advantage over the historian. As we construct our vision for the future, we realize that the future can be invented or designed. Believe it: our personal vision for mission is influential in shaping the future of the world.

I believe the health care reform issue is a perfect example of how we can construct the future from the past and the present. "Wellness" will be the new and the real health care revolution. Self-care will be the new mantra of the twenty-first century. The massive consolidation and restructuring that are overtaking our health care industry will focus on the true determinants of health and wellness—lifestyle, physical environment, housing, education, recreation, community, social structure, spiritual well-being. A major shift is under way, not just in managed care, not just in matters of curing illnesses, but in achieving and maintaining high-level well-being.

Is wellness an unrealistic dream? I don't think so. In fact, the ways in which society regulates and shapes its employment and economic policies, provides education, assists people in times of difficulty, finds solutions to poverty, crime, drug abuse, and other social ills will have as much—or more—impact on our health care system as do the resources being invested today in the detection, diagnosis, and treatment of illness. Wellness—in its broadest definition—is our future.

*Our personal
vision for mission
is influential in shaping
the future
of the world.*

GETTING BACK TO WHERE
WE STARTED

Crafting our personal vision takes a spark of genius, a transcending ability, a kind of magic that allows us to assemble out of all the options a clearly articulated vision of the future. This vision must be at once simple, easily understood, clearly desirable, and energizing. It must also be achievable and credible in terms of its time boundaries. Many visions are expressed in terms of ten-year goals, a time frame long enough to permit truly dramatic change yet one that is still within the comprehension and aspiration of our thinking.

Underlying vision is this question: "Who am I?" The answer: each of us must see himself or herself as a person of significance, a person who has, or can attain, the competency needed to carry out this vision.

Who am I? A child of God, filled with potential and with a willingness to start where I am and then build, change, and contribute. I am a person with a great vision!

Molding a vision consists mostly of a series of judgment calls. We can suggest here only some of the questions that should be addressed. They include the following:

1. Who are the people who have a stake in my future, and what is it that they would like to see happen?
2. What are the possible indicators of success in my vision for mission?
3. How can success be measured?
4. How would my vision unfold if I continued on my present path without any major changes?
5. What societal warning signs are now in place or are predictable that will affect my vision for mission?

6. What might I do to alter the course of events? What might be the consequences of my actions?
7. What resources do I now possess or can I obtain that will shape my vision for mission?
8. Of all the alternative possible visions for the future, which are more likely to be favorable to my survival, to my success, and to my real contribution to the world?

Questions such as these, and others, help you clarify your vision. They suggest viable alternatives. Synthesizing this information into a single vision is an art form. But we are all capable of doing so. This synthesis simply involves a degree of judgment, intuition, and creativity.

SEEKING GUIDANCE

I believe we have all been endowed with a deeper intelligence, a superconsciousness, an Inner Wisdom that equates to a higher power. This is the infinitely wise aspect of our being that simply "knows." Many people call it intuition.

This Inner Wisdom is really not complicated or mysterious. It is a natural endowment that comes to us through our intuitive senses, our "gut" feelings. As events unfold in our lives, all we need to do is pay attention to our reactions. For example, perhaps we're considering a career change. It is not uncommon for a fearful inner voice to speak up at such a time. But if we listen further, we will also often hear an excited voice saying, "Make the change. Everything will be just fine."

Our Inner Wisdom is always trying to help us bring balance and true fulfillment into our lives. I believe it is constructive, as long as we take the time to listen to it. Posing a question like "What direction do I need to take in my life right now?" is the key to opening ourselves up to answers that come from our Inner Wisdom.

Once you have posed the question, relax quietly and make a special effort to be open and receptive. Take note of the thoughts, feelings, and images that come to you in response to the question you have asked. Note also the words and actions of the people with whom you have contact. These may offer another form of response. Evaluate this guidance.

If no answer comes immediately, simply let the question go for the moment. I will often experience a special clarity on a particular issue after a night's sleep. Simply remain open for guidance. It invariably presents itself. We must simply notice.

(For a more in-depth understanding of how to find and develop your Inner Wisdom, refer to Appendix A.)

TAKING ACTION

It now remains to translate this vision into action. Visions are only as powerful as the ideas they communicate. The task implied in your vision for mission can be expressed in this way: I have seen who I can be. Now I must act to make it so.

This means commitment. A vision makes a difference only when it has been successfully communicated to the mind, emotion, and spirit of the individual and effectively assimilated as a guiding life principle. Then we begin to personify our vision.

J. Erik Jonsson was fascinated with science and technology. At fourteen years old, he bought an old two-cylinder motorcycle with money he saved from doing odd jobs. By trial and error he taught himself to keep the aging machine running.

Jonsson's fascination with science and technology led him to help found, build, and lead one of America's most powerful Fortune 500 companies, Texas Instruments. Texas Instruments' accomplishments in the semiconductor field dramatically advanced the development of that market.

In 1964, Jonsson was contemplating retirement when he was approached to fill out the balance of the term of the mayor of Dallas, who had resigned to run for a seat in Congress. Jonsson accepted, intending to serve only the remaining fifteen months of the term. But he stayed on for three more terms—seven years in all.

"It is action that makes the difference," said Jonsson. "No matter what the vision, it must come to the point where we simply do our best and get the job done." Jonsson personified the commitment needed to put a vision for mission into action.

A vision of the future is not defined once and for all and then put in a notebook never to be referred to again. For it to become real, we must recommit to it time and time again. It must become incorporated into our very being. It must be reinforced through decision-making processes.

————————

I
have seen
who
I can be.

I
must act
to make
it so.

————————

It must be constantly evaluated for change in the light of new circumstances.

And in the end, our vision must be implemented. Expressing it first in language that fires the imagination as well as the emotions and that empowers us to get things done—that is the key.

In the process, the answer to our question, "Who am I?" will take on a wonderfully new and different answer. Let us dedicate ourselves to the quest.

Guidance for Vision

1. Become responsible for fulfilling an ongoing assignment: to spend time each day in quiet and conscious solitude. Your single goal during this time is to hear what your Inner Wisdom has to say to you.

Be at peace. Listen. Be open to suggestion, to receiving wisdom and insight.

Minimize what you have to say. This is not traditional prayer. You are now listening. Listen with your heart and your mind. Keep this discipline twice daily. Concentrate on and record what your Inner Wisdom wants to get across to you. It is your spirit of openness that is paramount.

The importance of these messages in discovering your life mission cannot be overstated. When the messages start coming, jot them down so that they will not be lost to you. It is not enough to commit these messages to memory. Keep paper and pen with you, even at your bedside. Insights come at times other than your quiet period, often when you least expect it. Record them immediately. Spend time analyzing them.

2. Learn to distinguish between these inspired thoughts and your own. Use this basic guide: if the thought is free from an overwhelming personal desire, believe that it comes from your Inner Wisdom. Recognize that the thought needs to be tested—more on that later in Appendix A. If, on examination, the thought is controlled solely by some personal desire, discard it.

As these thoughts flow through you, try constantly to get yourself out of the picture. You will experience a sense of waves flowing into your mind; this is God's mind flowing into yours. Look for the sense of quiet strength and peace that confirms that these are the inspired words of God. Record each impression in turn. Prepare to test them later.

3. Carry a sense of gratitude with you into the world. Express thanks for the way you are being blessed at all times. You are blessed right now, even if you are facing your deepest adversity. Raise your awareness. As you become more aware of the riches God gives you constantly, you will see them expand. Gratitude begets abundance. Express your gratitude.

4. Study. Make books that are of comfort to you part of your daily regime. Seek constantly to deepen your spiritual understanding. Inspiring materials that God has sent through other men and women can offer guidance and uplift your spirit.

5. Sharpen your understanding of your vision. Give thoughtful consideration to each of the following prompts:

a. If I could wave a wand and know I could not fail, I would . . .

_____

_____

_____

b. At the end of my life, I would like to look back and know that I did something positive about . . .

_____

_____

_____

c. I would keep talking late into the night about the exciting topic(s) of . . .

_____

_____

_____

d. If my name were mentioned to a group of my friends, they would say I was really passionate about and interested in . . .

_____

_____

_____

6. Based on these responses, I sense I have a vision for . . .

_____

_____

_____

_____

_____

JUST THE BEGINNING

As you consider your answers and the direction you receive from your Inner Wisdom, take a moment to record the responses. Review them often. Your vision will begin to become clear.

2

SERVICE

You cannot sincerely help another without helping yourself.

Emerson

...

VISION + *SERVICE* × PASSION = MISSION

■ ■ ■

What makes for greatness?

"I keep discovering the power of God in my life when I do things for other people."

That's Robert J. Brown talking. He was born in Highpoint, North Carolina, the great-grandson of a slave. "When it rained, we put buckets all over the place, and the house was cold a lot because it was just an old house that Mama had bought with her earnings as a maid for the Southern Railroad."

Bob and his brother were reared by a grandmother who would pray every morning that God would help them rise above their circumstances in order to be helpful to others. "It was like it was being embedded into me and I grew up with it. Every day she would remind me of her basic philosophy of helping others."

His grandmother was a woman whose actions matched her beliefs. One incident stands out. When Bob Brown was just a youngster, an old man came by and said to his grandmother, "Miss Nellie, I'm hungry. I haven't had anything to eat in two days."

Bob watched his grandmother invite the man in and feed him in their own kitchen. The irony was, the Browns did not have enough food for themselves.

After the man left, Brown asked, "Mama, why do you feed all these old people who come off the street like this? Especially when we don't have anything."

"Bobbie," said his grandmother, motioning him to come up and sit beside her, "if I never teach you anything else, remember that what you got is not your own. It belongs to the Lord, and the Lord wants us to share it with others."

Robert Brown's legacy from his grandmother was a fundamental truth that is also the second requirement of the quest for life mission: service to others.

Service is synonymous with contributing to the welfare of others. Looking out for number one may be the fashion; certainly it is by most people's standards. But lending a hand has never gone out of style. That's because altruism has always had a lot going for it. It is never more crucial than when it comes to mission.

The late Hans Selye, M.D., who was responsible for the early studies tying stress to illness, called the concept of service "altruistic egoism." Through his years of study he, along with many other prominent scientists, came to recognize that giving of ourselves to others is an effective antidote to stress, as well as a pathway to health.

Robert Brown put his legacy to the test. He was a good student and won a scholarship his freshman year at Virginia Union University. He returned to Highpoint and started a public relations company. When the business began to prosper, he started to spend more time in the civil rights movement and traveled with the late Dr. Martin Luther King Jr. to raise money for the cause. Service was his guidepost.

In 1968, Brown was appointed special assistant to then President Richard M. Nixon. He started and developed the

U.S. Minority Enterprise Program and helped educate thousands with his U.S. government black college program. It has been said that Robert Brown, in his White House days, was responsible for channeling over a billion dollars to African-American colleges and businesses, as well as towns in the South.

Says Brown, "You have to become what I call a 'tenth miler.' If anybody wants you to go an extra mile, in terms of hard work, go ten miles, and most of the time you're not going to have anyone even close to you."

A major part of Bob Brown's life revolves around giving to the poor. He and his wife have put many needy kids through school. He is president of the International Concern Foundation, established to channel support from the private sector to the disadvantaged. Brown is the only American who visited Nelson Mandela during his twenty-seven years of imprisonment. He arranged full scholarships for Mandela's daughter and her husband to attend Boston University.

"Service is the key. I am grateful," said Brown, "that I've been able to utilize the resources that God has placed before me to be helpful to family, to be helpful to a lot of friends, and many other poor people who came out of the same circumstances I did."

Alice Gaither feels the same gratitude. High blood pressure can be one of the unwelcome side effects of her high-tension customer service job. Alice is director of customer services—"flak catcher"—for one of the nation's largest telecommunications firms. "I can handle any complaint as long as I keep the mental discipline to understand that it is an opportunity for me to serve." Alice says her blood pressure is fine. In fact, everything is fine. She's fit, doesn't lose sleep worrying, and "my kids like me."

In her spare time, Alice works with disadvantaged youth, raises money for a children's home, and has donated more than twelve gallons of blood to the American Red Cross. All in all, she says, "I'm a pretty happy girl."

When Arnold White was a child, they called him "Spaz." He grew up believing they were right. But a music teacher knew Arnold had athletic interests; he just hadn't been able to demonstrate them. And Arnold knew that he wanted to help people. Several years ago, he helped sponsor a local Special Olympics program for developmentally disabled youth. His participation gave Arnold a different opinion of himself.

"This gives me a sense of worth I never had before," he said. "It's like therapy that works both ways." And he noticed something even more remarkable. "I have arthritis," he explains, "and when I lose myself in helping those kids, it seems to make the pain go away."

Arnold White, and his wife Alice, are more than just a couple of do-gooders. Their lives—full and healthy— illustrate a little-known corollary to the Golden Rule: doing unto others can do wonderful things unto you.

THE TAO OF GREATNESS

While greatness tends to be different in its specifics for each person, and allowing that greatness does not equate with perfection, the best way we can fulfill—in fact the only way of fulfilling—our highest vision for mission potential is through service to others. It's the attitude and action of service that makes the difference.

When I was in the very depths of attempting to survive metastatic lung cancer, a friend gave me a powerful perspective. He said, "Greatness lies not in our duration but in our donation. Even in this hour of fear, focus on your donations."

Today, after living over twelve years after a terminal diagnosis and after dealing with literally thousands of people who have come through similar health crises, I am unequivocally convinced that service to others—our donations—has the ability to induce health.

Service is at the heart of Roger Burtonelli's dramatic recovery. Diagnosed with metastatic lymphoma, Roger was confined to his bedroom and was receiving daily home nursing care, including intravenous morphine in order to manage his pain. All the medical authorities concurred that he was in his end stage of life. Hospice care was begun.

I visited Roger and in the middle of our conversation felt led to ask, "How can you serve with this adversity?"

He was puzzled. I continued, "You are a person of deep wisdom. Have you thought about sharing that with others?"

Roger was silent. "What do you have in mind?" he finally asked slowly and deliberately.

"I can't be sure," I replied. "But let me ask you, have you shared the lessons you've learned in your rich and full life with your grandchildren?"

What happened next is something that I have seen repeatedly in people who catch a vision of their mission through service to others.

*Greatness
lies not
in our
duration
but in our
donation.*

Roger was silent. He pondered the implications of what we were discussing. Gradually, his face brightened. I watched his skin color go from an ashen gray to a more vibrant and healthy pink. He sat up straighter in the bed. His whole demeanor began to shift. He smiled a little. Roger held his head high. He raised his arm as he spoke.

"I could write them letters," he said as he nodded. "That's something I'm able to do."

Roger began to focus his thoughts and efforts on serving, on doing for others. His vision for mission was to pass along some of his wisdom to his children and grandchildren. He decided that his best strategy was writing.

Each letter addressed one subject. The first one was on persistence. The next, on the value of reading. Another on how to handle failure.

Roger began to feel better.

He would send copies of the letters to me for my critique. I particularly liked the one on his religious beliefs. Roger didn't tell people to believe in God. No. Roger told people that God believed in them. "And God's belief in us," wrote Roger, "requires our response."

Roger needed less morphine. He started to eat again.

I telephoned Roger after receiving another of his letters. "I think God has a plan for me right here in these letters," said Roger. "This isn't labor, it's play."

Today, Roger's doctors call his recovery a miracle. If you talk to Roger about why he is still alive, he'll certainly credit medical care as playing a significant role. He'll also quickly give accolades to his wife and family for their unwavering support. But when you allow Roger to speak from his heart, he will say the reason he is alive today is because he caught hold of a mission. He decided to serve.

GIVING AND RECEIVING HEALTH

The biblical phrase, "As ye sow, so shall ye reap," seems all the more true when applied to service. Service has some valuable paybacks: the love and gratitude we inspire in those we help, the increase in our own self-esteem, and the positive change in our own physiology.

George Vaillant, M.D., psychologist and director of a forty-year study of Harvard graduates, identified service as "one of the qualities that help even the most poorly adjusted men of the study group deal successfully with the stresses of life. It's service that makes the difference."

In fact, the opposite of service, selfishness, may make us ill. Larry Scherwitz, Ph.D., thinks it might. A social psychologist at the Medical Research Institute of San Francisco, Dr. Scherwitz turned up a startling fact in a major study on coronary artery disease: people who used the pronouns *I, me,* and *my* most often in an interview were more likely to develop coronary heart disease than those who made fewer references to themselves—even when other health-threatening behaviors were controlled. Dr. Scherwitz summed it up: "The more self-centered people were much more likely to die of heart attack than the less self-centered."

Dean Ornish, M.D., author of *Reversing Heart Disease,* concurs: "The exaggerated focus on the self may further reinforce the sense of isolation and separateness." In other words, looking out for number one is not enlightened self-interest at all. It's just lonely. It is selfish. And selfishness, and the accompanying loneliness, kills.

Grasp it. Service is an essential part of mission. We've long known that people with generous spirits tend to be happier, but now science is confirming that they're healthier and live longer, too. Generosity comes naturally to us, but only if we let it. *Give* is a four-letter word spelled h-e-l-p.

James Lynch, Ph.D., a leading specialist in psychosomatic medicine, documented the connection between caring and heart disease. He says, "The mandate to 'love your neighbor as you love yourself' is not just a moral mandate. It is a psychological mandate. Caring is biological." It has an effect on the whole body.

Through my own work on wellness among the elderly, I met an eighty-five-year-old who volunteers frequently and who expresses the benefits in this way: "Serving others helps me keep well so that I can keep giving. Serving others is a blessing. It wards off old age."

Alfred N. Larsen, national director of the Retired Senior Volunteer Program (RSVP), agrees. His organization has placed thousands of elderly people in community volunteer jobs. He is convinced that serving others is of high value to the elderly, particularly those who lose family, friends, and often a sense of purpose as they grow older.

Service keeps you young, healthy, and alive.

THE IMPORTANCE OF INTENT

The benefits of service go far beyond health. Every relationship that is part of our lives—spouse, child, employer, employee, friend, institution—involves give and take, serving and being served. What goes up must come down; what we give, we receive. It's karma.

In every seed lies the promise of new life. But the seed must not be hoarded; it must be given to the fertile ground so that it can grow. Once the seed is given, an unseen energy serves to translate the promise of growth into a material reality.

So, too, with service. It is the intention behind our giving, and our receiving, that is of critical importance. The intention should always be to create happiness for the giver and for yourself.

The return we receive from our service is directly proportional to the giving when we give unconditionally and from the heart. The act of service must be joyful. We must feel joy in the very act of giving itself, not just in the potential return. Joyful giving increases the energy that service creates many times over.

Alcoholics Anonymous (AA) is perhaps one of the best working examples of the principle of "When I help you, I help me." AA, not incidentally, is one of the most powerful forces for spiritual transformation in this century. Its twelve-step program offers some of the most concentrated and effective self-help wisdom in the world.

But self-help, with its implications of individual effort, is actually a misnomer; what AA offers is mutual help. Members of AA are helped by helping others. They are served by serving.

This idea must not be dismissed. When we serve, we give one another a special kind of human companionship.

*The
intention behind
service:
create happiness
for both
ourselves
and the
receiver.*

When people share their problems and search for solutions together, there is a strong sense of connectedness and of mutual understanding.

Our work with the Cancer Conquerors Foundation, a mutual-support group that specializes in the integration of body, mind, and spirit, proves that service to others literally can be a form of health care. Group members reinforce their own good health habits and positive attitudes by sharing their advice and practices with others.

Serving people by helping others in the same boat is literally practicing a survival skill. Lending a helping hand makes the vulnerable new cancer patient feel less vulnerable. Helping others is a way of regaining control over one's own health and life. But there is one proviso.

The return from this giving depends wholly on the act of service being joyful.

We all want to be happy and healthy and live a long life. Does this mean that we should march right out like Bob Brown, Alice Gaither, and Arnold White and devote our lives to national service or give a pint of blood or help with the Special Olympics? No, not if you're only giving in order to get something in return. The only way a giver can reap the full benefits of service to others is if the service comes out of the goodness in his or her heart, and not out of the need.

We cannot expect a return of goodies if we're not sincerely serving. If the person we've served doesn't thank us and we get angry, we're not serving with integrity. We've become too attached to the fruits of our labor.

This was brought home to me vividly at a time when I was serving in downtown Los Angeles. As I left my car in a parking lot each day, I would pass a long line of homeless men. Invariably, they would hold out a cup or ask for a quarter.

One day I prepared two tuna fish sandwiches to give to one of the men. The sandwiches were nutritious, prepared with whole wheat bread and fresh crispy lettuce. I knew this was the right thing to do. Instead of money, I'd give someone something to eat.

I proudly put the sandwiches in a clear plastic bag, slipped a napkin underneath, and tied it with a twisty. As I left the parking lot, I was prepared to give them to the first person who asked for money.

I wasn't disappointed. The second person I saw yelled, "Hey, mister, you gotta spare quarter?"

I walked over to him, proudly presented the two tuna fish sandwiches, and said, "I hope you'll enjoy a good meal."

He looked at the bag of sandwiches, gave it to the man standing next to him, and shouted to the next person coming down the sidewalk, "Hey, buddy, can you spare a quarter?"

I wanted to scream, "Hey, where's your gratitude? Why don't you eat those? What's wrong with you?" But as a friend later reminded me, service must be offered without any conditions.

No conditions. I had to examine my motives and consider my own needs. I had expected some appreciation, maybe even some recognition and positive reinforcement. What I uncovered were the hidden conditions that I had attached to helping another person. I was surprised; I had

*Feel joy
in the very act
of service,
not
in the
expected return.*

been operating out of my own need, out of a need for my ego to be stroked. I learned a great deal from that experience. The big lesson: feel joy in the very act of service, not in the expected return.

THE LAW OF RECIPROCITY

The concept of fulfilling your mission through service is actually very simple, but it is not simplistic:

What you want to receive, give to others.

If you want love, learn to give love. If you want attention or appreciation, learn to give attention and appreciation. If you want joy and happiness, learn to give joy and happiness. If you want abundance, help others find abundance. Service is the mind-set.

Giving others what you want is the simplest way to get your own needs met. This master principle of mission works equally well for individuals, organizations, and nations.

One of the leaders of our Cancer Conquerors support groups wrote, "I wanted wellness. I received it only when I was able to help others know wellness." Yes, that's it.

Service is one of those timeless laws of cause and effect that operate in the world of personal effectiveness and human interaction. Service is part of the great collective wisdom of the ages. It is a recurring theme, found at the heart of every truly great person or society. Service governs the entire quality of our lives. In the long run—and provided our intent is pure—only if we focus on service will we know happiness and the quality of life that is its result.

Reciprocity is a natural result whenever service occurs. In a real sense, the essence of working toward your mission is all about putting into effect the whole system of service and reciprocity, giving and receiving. When we set this in motion, miracles begin to happen.

Jean Nidetch was a 214-pound New York housewife and mother when she formed what was to become the first Weight Watchers group. In 1961, Jean invited six overweight friends to meet weekly in her Queens apartment. They would talk about their mutual problem and support one another through the rigors of dieting.

Nidetch's intent was pure. Jean had no thought that this small group could become the forerunner of a business enterprise. She knew only that the support of friends in similar circumstances might help her lose weight and keep it off for the first time in her life.

"I realized that what I needed was to talk to someone who could give me feedback," Jean said. "And if I needed it, others needed it just as much."

In the early 1960s when support groups were nonexistent and the self-help movement was a floundering baby, Nidetch's idea struck a chord in those who heard about it. The initial group grew rapidly. Within three months, forty people were squeezing into her modest apartment for a weekly meeting and the opportunity to speak openly and honestly with others about weight problems.

"The only requirement we had for attendance," said Jean, "was that everyone had to bring her own chair!"

Over the next year, she started to lead similar groups throughout the New York metropolitan area. In May of

1963, at a trim 132 pounds, she incorporated and rented a loft in Queens to hold the first public Weight Watchers meeting.

Jean Nidetch's intent remained pure; Weight Watchers was focused on service. That initial meeting in the loft was not advertised, but Nidetch told members of her existing groups about the gathering. To her astonishment, some four hundred people were waiting outside the loft when she arrived in the morning.

Service remained the key. "I panicked," admits Jean. "I still get goose bumps when I think about it. I don't know if you've ever seen over four hundred fat people in one place, but I hadn't. The need for what we were doing was so great."

Since she had rented only fifty chairs, Nidetch and a friend, whom she recruited from that very line as her assistant, spent that day meeting people in groups of fifty, with the waiting assembly standing in the street.

Thus was born Weight Watchers. In the years since, more than fifty million people worldwide have enrolled in the program. Today, Weight Watchers International is a wholly owned subsidiary of the H. J. Heinz Company, and it is a billion-dollar business with over forty-four thousand employees in nearly thirty countries. It all started with service.

The best way to start exploring the sense of mission in your own life is to make a conscious decision to serve. Start small. Decide that anytime you come into contact with anyone you will give that person something.

With our intent pure—giving simply to bring joy to ourselves and others and not because we hope for a return—we set into motion an entire system of service and reciprocity.

Anytime
you come
into contact
with anyone,
give
that person
something.

Just start! When you do, you will garner assets that can help you weather the storms of life. It's as if you store up these good feelings for the bad times, in much the same way squirrels put away food for the winter.

The decision to give something to every person we come into contact with reminds us that although everything else might be going badly, *we* are not. This knowledge can give us a sense of self-esteem, of power and control. And from these good feelings we will begin to reap the rewards.

UNLIMITED OPPORTUNITIES TO SERVE

A hobby can offer an opportunity for service. Lee Flaherty was an avid long-distance runner. In 1977, Flaherty founded the Chicago Marathon and still assists in managing the event. The annual marathon, which is televised, attracts over fifteen thousand runners, a million spectators, and hundreds of journalists from around the world.

"It's a great opportunity to show what Chicago is all about," says Flaherty. "Each year this is a big festival in this town. My hobby turned out to be something I can do for the city of Chicago."

Make the decision to serve. The service we offer does not have to take the form of material things; a smile, a compliment, some encouragement, or a prayer is often the most appropriate gift.

In fact, the most powerful forms of service are nonmaterial. The gifts of pure caring, true attention, unconditional affection, sincere appreciation, and unconditional love are some of the most powerful forms of service in the world. They don't cost a dime! It's the pure intent that gives them power.

When you meet someone, you can silently send them one of these true blessings. Wish them bliss and joy. The power behind this type of service is elegant and significant.

This does not mean we never give a material gift. My wife is wonderful in her dedication to offering small gifts to people. We simply do not go to another couple's home without taking something; we don't make a visit without a gift. Maybe it's something as simple as a fresh flower from our garden, or perhaps it's a book of poetry. She recently copied a verse of Scripture and sent it along with a note to a person who is hurting. You can bring a compliment. You can bring a prayer. There is always something to give.

Make the decision to serve wherever you go and to whomever you see. As long as you are serving, you will be receiving. The more you serve, the more confidence you will gain in the miraculous effects of this principle of life. And as you enjoy the reciprocity, your ability to serve will also increase.

Service begins with the initiative of the individual. The forces of good and evil in this world are propelled by the thoughts, attitudes, and actions of you and me. Service is critically important, not just for us personally but also for the quality of our society and our world in the future. The concepts that each individual brings to service help to shape our world as it is being born each day.

Truett Cathy is a person with a deep sense of service that began with his personal initiative. Founder of the Atlanta-based Chick-Fil-A, the nation's fourth largest chicken franchise, Cathy built the entire company around dedication to service of both customers and employees. While it is common for organizations to focus on customer service, the depth of Cathy's concern for his restaurant operators and crew members is exceptional. Innovative incentive programs and a unique scholarship program are the highlights of his commitment.

"It's important in business to pay attention to your cash flow," says Cathy, "but more important to pay attention to your people flow. It's people who make a company succeed or fail. We are very conscious of that truth."

The fast-food industry is notorious for high employee turnover. Chick-Fil-A boasts the industry's lowest rate. Today, more than twelve thousand young people work in Chick-Fil-A restaurants, motivated in part by the promise of a thousand-dollar scholarship for those who work an average of twenty hours per week for two years. There's also the ability to compete annually with other Chick-Fil-A workers for four-year scholarships of ten thousand dollars.

"I tell our people that getting a scholarship from Chick-Fil-A is not just important for the money," says Cathy, "it also looks outstanding on your résumé. It shows that even as a young person, you demonstrated dependability and stability."

THE POWER OF SERVICE

Service is fundamentally powerful. It is true that perhaps only a few people will receive this insight. And perhaps even fewer will act on it. But if we truly seek to fulfill our life mission, then we must act on the service insight. And the world can learn from our example.

Service is important at every level. A mother in South Central Los Angeles loses a daughter to street violence. In her grief, she asks, "What can I do?" Her Inner Wisdom tells her, "Start a youth outreach."

She does. With no building, no facilities, and no equipment, she begins to hold meetings regularly under a tree in her front yard. Elementary and middle school students respond. Today, after-school programs exist in six different churches in South Central Los Angeles because of her efforts. It all started with a decision to serve.

Fulfilling your mission through service is the essence of leadership. It means that you are willing to go out ahead, to show the way, to be open to the unusual, to follow inspiration.

Service transforms your sense of mission and attracts followers. Other lives are touched. Others see more clearly what is best because of our example of service. Our task is to put the law of service and reciprocity into effect daily, not just to help ourselves but to show the way for others.

Vow to serve. Make a decision that wherever you go and whomever you encounter, you will bring them a gift. Let it be a gift of encouragement or a compliment; give a gift of your belief in the other person.

Give the gift of prayer, the gift of trust, the gift of accountability, knowing that only when we hold ourselves accountable to give back can we also hold others accountable.

If you've ever stayed at a Days Inn, you have been touched by Deen Day Smith and her philosophy of giving back. "I work ten or twelve hours a day," she says, "just about every day, usually on community activities." Deeply involved in the planning of the spectacular 1996 Summer Olympics in Atlanta, her interest is in bringing people of various races and cultures together.

"If you've been blessed abundantly, you must be willing to volunteer and give back to the people who helped get where you are." Her late husband, Cycil, founded Days Inn of America. She helped expand the chain. After his death, Deen sold the organization. She recalls, "We distributed a check to employees who had been with us, such as a maid or a cook, the people who are not usually remembered. I believe that when people invest in your life to make it better for you personally, you should also make it better for them. That's my understanding of 'trickle-down' economics."

Follow that example. Give back. Serve everyone with whom you come in contact. Then note how the law of reciprocity works again and again to compensate you.

Gratefully receive all the gifts that return. This is life offering you confirmation of your mission.

Receive with thanks the gifts we take for granted—those of sunlight, and the sounds of birds singing, or spring showers, or even the first snow of winter. Be open to receiving from others, whether it be in the form of compliments, encouragement, or even a material gift.

Make service the center of your conscious activities, rather than an occasional or random act. Service needs to become the very lifeblood of the process of fulfilling one's mission. It's not that spur-of-the-moment demonstrations of kindness are wrong. It's simply that we cannot fulfill our mission by waiting until it "feels right."

As nice as it is to put coins in expired parking meters or to give away a bouquet of flowers you had meant to take home to your own dinner table, a sense of mission requires us to cultivate service on a much deeper level.

*The conscious and
systematic development
of service as a
guiding principle
results in both
success and significance.*

I admire the work of author Steven Covey. In his several books, including *The Seven Habits of Highly Effective People* and *First Things First,* he urges us to focus on principle-centered living. Good advice.

But let's become exceedingly clear on one important point. I submit that the single greatest principle of one's life mission is service. This implies that as you seek to fulfill your mission, whatever it may be, you will consciously culti-vate active service to others *as a way of life.* This conscious cultivation is something that we must practice at home, in our marriages, in our parenting, and at our work, as individ-uals and as nations. It is the conscious and systematic de-velopment of service as a guiding principle that results in both success and significance. We simply cannot wait until a spontaneous impulse to serve moves us.

Most of us do reasonably well in our efforts to serve. We fulfill our obligations by being responsible parents, assisting our colleagues at work, supporting our spouses, doing our best to serve in our communities.

But these expectations are just that—what we're *expected* to do. In fact, we have agreed to serve in this way because of the mates we have chosen or the lives we've decided to live. This sort of basic and fundamental service comes with the territory, so to speak. As people of reasonable civility, we serve just by meeting our daily responsibilities.

Fulfilling our mission requires us to take steps that are out of the ordinary. One of the most touching stories I have heard about service and mission was told by an anonymous Vietnam war veteran. His company had gone into a Vietcong village and ransacked the entire place. They had found nothing. As they left the village and started up a trail, they were ambushed. Our veteran was severely wounded.

The next thing he remembered, he woke up with a very old Vietnamese woman leaning over him. As he slipped back into unconsciousness, he remembered thinking that surely he was about to die. But he woke again to find that his wound had been cleaned and bandaged, and the woman was leaning over him again offering a cup of hot tea.

As our American soldier was sipping the tea and attempting to understand how and why he was still alive, the sound of a helicopter was heard. It had come to take him back. Just as the helicopter landed, the old woman quietly got up and disappeared into the underbrush.

Let this example of service touch your soul. This true story of giving even to those who would destroy our lives exemplifies the attitude we must cultivate in order to live out our mission.

This level of service is not just the result of spontaneity or an example of once-in-a-while compassion. That Vietnamese woman demonstrated the highest level of personal greatness in her dedication to service.

The same capacity exists in each of us. Everyone reading these words has loved someone. Everyone has done someone a kindness, has healed a wound, has taken on an assignment without being asked, has created something of beauty and shared it with others.

Our mission unfolds as we make this passion for service the guiding principle in our life, for then we move beyond the confines of our routine daily human condition, and we stir the part of us that is divine.

Service sets the soul free to give for the sheer and exhilarating sake of giving. We serve not out of obligation but out of love—out of the necessity to act out our love.

Living out our mission is about changing the world, a world that makes us struggle, that makes us discouraged, that makes us weary. Service seeks to change the world into a kinder, gentler, sweeter place through our demonstrations of love.

Service. It changes the very atmosphere in which we live. Quietly, almost imperceptibly, our attitude and actions of service allow a song to break forth in our lives. The world is eager for its melody.

"I spent a lifetime establishing that there are no disabled people, only people with varying degrees of abilities," says Henry J. Viscardi Jr., founder and president of the National Center for Disability Services.

Viscardi's experience is a symphony of service to others. He spent the first six years of his life in a hospital where "they tried to straighten out the crooked little stumps with which I was born." It wasn't until Viscardi was twenty-seven years old that he was fitted with artificial limbs. "For the first time," he says, "I stood up tall and straight and faced a whole new life. I was no longer the object of pity or ridicule, and what a joy it was to see the top of my mother's head, to wind the clock on the mantel, to have my sister teach me how to dance."

Henry Viscardi helped establish Just One Break, a New York–based free employment service for the disabled. This was followed in 1952 by Abilities, forerunner of today's National Center for Disability Services.

His service has changed America and is changing the world. Viscardi reflects on how different his own experience was. "When I was a crippled boy going to school, I was excused from science because I couldn't climb up on the stool. The lab tables were so high I couldn't reach the microscopes. And, of course, I was excused from gym."

Today, the results of Henry Viscardi's efforts can be seen everywhere. He is the author of eight books, has advised United States presidents, served as chairman of the White House Conference on Handicapped Individuals, and received nineteen honorary doctorate degrees.

Service was at the core of this man's very being. Viscardi says it all started with a doctor who made a difference in his life. "When the stumps on which I was getting about were wearing out, he felt that I could be fitted with artificial limbs. However, I couldn't pay his bill. He told me if I would make the difference for one other life—a life dependent on the charity of family or the community compared to the life full of dignity and self-sufficiency—that his bill would be repaid. And I'm still paying that bill.

"I promised him and I pledge to the world that so long as there is one disabled individual who prefers the challenges of life to the guaranteed existence, I'll be standing at that individual's side as long as I can."

Service is the one true common human vocation. It is our great shared mission. Service connects us, centers us, binds us into one great spirit.

As we serve, we begin to understand that as we give we receive, as we bless we are blessed, and as we live out our mission, our mission gains power.

William Penn taught us of service when he said:

If there is any kindness I can show, or any good thing I can
do to any fellow being, let me do it now, and not deter or
neglect it, as I shall not pass this way again.

What makes for greatness? Indeed, it is recognizing that
the mission of life is to create a life of service. Service is the
measure of our success, the plumb line of our significance.
Serve. Now. You shall not pass this way again.

Guidance for Service

Consider the following prompts:

1. The issues and/or causes I feel strongly about are:

[] Literacy []Family []Technology

[] International Peace [] Racism [] Politics

[] Hunger [] Poverty [] Homosexuality

[] Addictions [] Injustice [] AIDS

[] Child care [] Abortion [] Health care

[] Economics [] Education [] Violence

[] Environment [] Spirituality [] Other _____

2. The people I would like to help most are:

[] Infants [] Children [] Youth

[] College students [] Teenage moms [] Single parents

[] Ill [] Elderly [] Unemployed

[] Disabled [] Poor [] Prisoners

[] Divorced [] Widowed [] Single people

[] Career trackers [] Refugees [] Newly married

[] Homeless [] Parents [] Empty nesters

3. What I envision myself doing for others is:

_____

_____

_____

4. I believe the area in which I could make the most significant contribution is:

_____

_____

_____

_____

_____

3

—————

PASSION

Be happy. It is a way of being wise.

Colette

—————————————
···

VISION + SERVICE × *PASSION* = MISSION

■ ■ ■

What makes for a joyful life?

Twenty-two million dollars! The woman hit the Lotto jackpot.

The year is 1988. Her family and friends are gathered around her. The television lights are blazing. Even the network news is there. She is ecstatic. "This," the woman proclaimed, "is the happiest day of my life!"

Fast-forward to 1993. The television lights are shining on this woman again. But tonight she is on *Hard Copy.* Her look is sullen. She's shaking her head in disbelief. What started out as the happiest time of her life has now turned on her.

In a matter of a few short years, she has gone through a divorce, the alienation of her children, and an investment that has turned sour. A judge has now garnished her lottery winnings for life. The closing scene shows the woman sitting on the steps of an apartment building in utter despair.

What makes for this elusive thing called happiness? What goes into the recipe for true and lasting joy? And what does it have to do with mission?

The happiest, most joyful person I know is a physically handicapped gentleman by the name of Lloyd Beamesderfer. Involved in a serious auto accident as a young man, Lloyd

*Joy
is independent
of our
circumstances.*

has spent a lifetime living with progressive disabilities. He recently went through an excruciating operation to relieve severe back pain. It didn't work and he is in even more discomfort. He now finds it necessary to use a motor-driven scooter in order to be mobile.

But this man exudes joy. People are drawn to Lloyd. Whenever you see him, which I do often, you receive a lift. His smile is genuine, his eyes loving and alive. His greeting is always positive; he affirms his guests. Lloyd invariably reaches out with both hands to give a loving handshake. And most people lean over to give him a big hug. His response is almost always an even bigger smile and affirming words such as "Oh, you've made my day."

Joy—it's the emotion evoked by well-being. It's delight and bliss we're talking about here, genuine happiness. But why is it so rare? And how can joy so quickly escape the person who has been declared the latest lottery winner but come naturally to people who have every reason to be bitter?

The name Lee Iacocca is synonymous with success and significance in the auto industry. First with Ford Motor Company, Iacocca was given, or took, credit for the introduction of the highly successful Ford Mustang. Fired by Henry Ford II, Iacocca ended up twice saving Chrysler from certain bankruptcy. He engineered approval for government-backed loans and paid them off early.

Iacocca was revered like a king. His commercials not only sold cars and minivans but also inspired the entire Chrysler workforce, instilling in them a new sense of pride and team spirit. Besides starring in his own television commercials, Iacocca wrote one of the best-selling business books of all time, raised millions to renovate the Statue of Liberty, and nearly managed to orchestrate a petition movement to get himself nominated for president. Not incidentally, all these activities made Iacocca a star.

Then comes retirement. Iacocca is miserable. In an interview with *Fortune* magazine, he shares that his three years of retirement have been hell. He laments a nasty and failed takeover bid for Chrysler, a second divorce, and his lonely life in the posh enclave of Bel Air, California. Since he still has millions in stock options, huge trust funds for his children, and a royal lifestyle, it's difficult to arouse much sympathy for Iacocca. But one thing is certain: he hasn't found happiness.

As we begin to ponder this thing called joy, some issues become clear right away. First, joy is independent of our circumstances. Just because you have the stock options doesn't mean you have a life. Dazzling professional exploits and bounteous wealth are no guarantee of happiness.

Search as people might, only a few discover in their lifetime this great truth about joyous living: joy is completely independent of what happens to you from the outside.

We search for joy in the wrong places. A classic story tells of a man searching under a streetlight in the dark of night. He is looking for a lost key. A stranger passes by and asks what the fellow is looking for. He responds, "My key." And the second man joins in the search.

After several minutes of unsuccessful searching, the second man asks the first, "Now tell me, exactly where were you standing when you dropped the key?"

"Oh, I was standing in the house," replied the first man, "but the electricity is off. So I came out here to search under the light of the street lamp."

The key isn't out there. It wasn't lost out there, and it will not be found out there. But oh, how that man tries to insist that it is there.

So, too, with joy. We seek it from the outside. But it comes from within. Understand the depths of this truth: no person or event or set of circumstances has any real power to make us happy.

This comes as a shock to most people. We spend a major portion of our lives waiting for circumstances and people to change so that things will get better for us—so that we can know happiness. Joy doesn't work that way.

Joy remains extremely elusive. Take a moment for a test. How many truly happy people do you know? Give this some thought. Answer the question honestly. Count out the number of people who, in your opinion, know deep joy in their lives. Use your fingers to count them. Unless you know very special people, your ten fingers will probably be adequate for the task.

JOY WITHIN

The story of Viktor Frankl powerfully demonstrates the truth that joy can be found only within.

The prisoners of the Nazi concentration camps during World War II, Viktor Frankl among them, had little reason to feel any joy, let alone hope, in their lives. They were stripped of their freedom, their dignity, their clothing. They were separated from their wives and husbands and children.

Viktor Frankl lost his wife, along with everything else. Yet his vivid recollections of the men who walked through the huts comforting others, giving away their last piece of bread, led him to develop what he later came to call "logotherapy." Frankl observed, "Everything can be taken from a man but one thing: to choose one's attitude in any given set of circumstances, to choose one's way."

Examine Frankl's insight—"to choose one's attitude in any given set of circumstances." Joy—or any attitude, for that matter—is a choice. If we keep looking to the people and events of our lives to fill our cups with joy, we will experience an unquenched thirst. To be satisfied, we will need circumstance after circumstance, person after person, adrenaline rush after adrenaline rush, new car after new car, bigger house after bigger house, more exotic vacation after more exotic vacation, more money, more power, more fame—and even then we will be receiving only temporary stimulation.

The chase to find happiness outside ourselves never results in lasting joy. But a look within opens the door.

The key to the doorway to happiness is honoring your passion. Passion is the intense driving emotional and spiritual connection with the process, not the object, of your deepest interest. Fervor. Vigor. Energy. Enthusiasm. Zeal. That's the stuff of passion.

Adding passion to our vision and our commitment to service animates our mission quest. In fact, passion doesn't just add to our sense of mission, it's a multiplying factor. Anyone can have a vision. And all people can serve. But it's when passion enters the equation that the magic results.

One of the singularly most successful people in the cut-throat world of corporate advertising is David Ogilvy. He is a believer in passion in the workplace. "Make it fun to work in your agency," he said. "When people aren't having any fun, they don't produce good advertising. Encourage exuberance. Get rid of the sad dogs who spread doom."

Ogilvy's words are jewels to be treasured. Often our energies are scattered or diffuse, but passion gathers all our creative powers together and focuses them on our objective, rather than away from it. Passion is indeed the multiplier; ten plus ten is twenty, but ten times ten is one hundred.

We must not wait for passion to be triggered by winning the lottery or having some other wonderful event happen in our life. If we count on something outside ourselves to turn passion on, then something else will be able to turn our passion off. Remember that living life with passion is a choice, an inside-out deal.

JOY AS A BIRTHRIGHT

Another realization in our search: we already possess passion and joy. We must simply choose it.

It strikes me as significant that here in the United States, our founding fathers thought true happiness was so important that they incorporated it into the framework of our society. Our Declaration of Independence affirms the right to joy. The document was written mostly by Thomas Jefferson. The key driving force of the entire formation of the United States is contained in these few words:

We hold these truths to be self-evident, that all men are created equal, that they are endowed by their Creator with certain unalienable rights, among these are life, liberty, and the pursuit of happiness. . . .

Happiness and joy are so fundamental to the human spirit that America's founding fathers thought it essential to guarantee it.

The framers of the Declaration of Independence recognized that true joy is actually part of our nature. Our task is simply to let it out. Joy and passion are built into our very being. They may be covered up by years of neglect, buried by the mundane chores of daily living. But passion is there, lurking just below the surface of our existence, awaiting our invitation, our release.

Even in the face of outer circumstances that can range from boring to dehumanizing, the experience of joy is always present within us.

"After I was raped," shared Lupe, a young and attractive woman, "I felt I would never know sanity again. It was as if a precious part of my soul had been stolen. When I reported it to the police, they accused me of provoking the incident. I felt shame."

Lupe (this is not her real name) had been attending one of our wellness support groups for nearly six months. She was painfully shy, hardly saying a word after the introductions. But she kept coming. This was the first time she publicly shared her nightmare.

With details too painful to repeat, Lupe told of being abducted from a parking lot at a shopping mall where she

_____

*We already
possess
joy.
We must
simply
let it out.*

━━━━━━━━━━━━

worked. Three men shoved her in the backseat of their car and sped away.

Lupe was forced to keep her head buried in the seat cushion. She cried and pleaded to be released. But the men, drunk and boisterous, began to beat her. She faded in and out of consciousness.

The rest was a horrifying ordeal. Lupe was driven to a remote area where the men had an old dilapidated cabin. She was blindfolded, gagged, stripped, and bound to a bed with gray duct tape. Over the next several hours, the men took turns repeatedly raping and sodomizing her. Before daylight, one of the men drove her to an even more remote area where he beat her with a tire iron and pushed her down a ravine. She was left for dead.

The group was speechless as Lupe continued. "But after three long years of serious inner work, I finally became able to trust again. I recognized that nobody could take away my happiness except me."

Lupe began volunteer work for a rape crisis hot line, trying to use that terrible experience for good. And through that work she began to heal. "I learned that joy is not something you take in," said Lupe, "but something that you let out."

JOY BEGINS WITH GRATITUDE

Joy is a decision that transcends any circumstance.

Kathy received a call from her husband. It was very brief: "Look for a letter underneath my things in the underwear drawer."

Trembling, Kathy opened the letter. She started to read. "If you are reading this letter, it will mean that I have managed to leave the country with a very large amount of money."

The letter went on to attempt to justify her husband's actions. He said he felt he was a great failure. He was looking for a way out. He wanted more. He offered a weak apology as he closed the letter:

> I know I have never brought you and the children happiness and joy. Without me here, now you'll have a chance to find it.

Kathy was devastated. Her children, ages six and four, were confused and hurt. The older child's teacher found the girl in tears and asked, "What's wrong?"

The reply: "Daddy's mad at me and won't come home."

How do you choose joy, how do you stir passion for life under such circumstances? Kathy, devoutly religious, decided that the best route was to practice counting her daily blessings. Keenly aware of her mission to raise her two young children into productive, loving human beings, Kathy made a decision based on an old hymn she had learned as a child: "Count your blessings; name them one by one."

A blessing is something for which you can be grateful. Like the tightrope walker who focuses just on the next step along the wire, Kathy made a conscious decision to focus on what she did have.

"At first," she said, "I tallied up my troubles and worries with the speed of an electronic calculator. That made me an expert in trouble counting. I decided I would become an expert in blessing counting."

With courage and with her heart and mind focused on her mission, Kathy made an inventory of her joys. For years she had been keeping a journal. She began a special page at the back of her journal and entitled it "My Joys." She started making a list:

1. I am thankful for life, my own and the lives of my two children.
2. I am thankful that I have this modest but clean home.
3. I am thankful we have enough to eat.
4. I am thankful we have clothes to wear.
5. I am thankful for my job and the opportunities it gives me.

Kathy added to her list daily. Nothing was too small or commonplace to be overlooked because, as she said, "I would miss these if I did not have them."

Kathy's focus was on what she had left and not what she had lost. Determined to carry out her mission with joy, she started by being grateful for all she did have.

JOY'S ENEMIES

Joy and passion are already ours; it waits within, awaiting our invitation to appear. It is a gift instilled in us at the moment of our conception. Like love, joy and passion are always a part of us, always waiting to be activated. But we don't have to wait for somebody else or some special event to throw our joy switch. We can activate it ourselves, not because of what's going on in our lives, not even in spite of what's going on in our lives, but simply because we exist.

Passion's greatest enemies are self-pity and worry. These two joy stealers are states of mind, and they are luxuries that the person who would fulfill his or her mission simply cannot afford.

Self-pity looks at life's circumstances and says, "I am not able to respond." Self-pity is a "life isn't fair" attitude that bogs people down, destroys initiative, and saps self-confidence. Self-pity trades in the currency of comparison: "He gets all the breaks." "She comes from a family of means." "I can't match his accomplishments because I don't have his education."

The person who decides to live out his or her life mission has no room for self-pity. We must start where we are and be willing, even passionate, about the contribution we can make here and now. Comparison with others has no constructive place in our being; when we compare, it should be only to judge our own progress against our previous efforts.

Worry is an even more prevalent joy stealer. You and I were not born with worry; we acquired it. It is a mental habit taken on from other people.

Because worry is a habit, it can be cast out of our mind and replaced with passion.

I spoke to a group of medical professionals on how the worry cycle can trigger negative physiological responses. We were examining the role of chronic worry in inhibiting immune function. Afterward, an oncologist came up to me and said, "Do you know what I do to chase worry away? I chop wood."

He had my attention. I asked him to tell me more.

"When I need to break through my worries, I go out into the dense woods behind our house and look for trees that would make good firewood. As I start to work on that tree, sawing, using the ax, engaging the log splitter, I see my troubles and worries start to untangle.

"It's like I need to occupy myself with something other than worry in order for the joy to break back through. For me to get on track again, I have to get off track for a while. Invariably," he concluded, "the results are amazing."

True passion and real joy come when we know we can trust, no matter what the outcome, that any circumstance can be used for good. We can be permanently free from self-pity and worry, allowing that inner joy to be set free.

William James, the great psychologist, gave us one of the keys to breaking the worry habit. He said, "The essence of genius is to know *what* to overlook." When we overlook the mental habit of worry and when we focus on accomplishing our mission, we stop wasting energy; as a result, joy can bubble forth from within.

I consider myself an expert at managing worry. My mother was a world-champion worrier, and I recognized early on that I needed to break this destructive habit. Worry actually creates a self-perpetuating cycle. So when worry starts to bog me down, I take the following helpful steps:

First, I acknowledge that worry is a habitual way of responding to life. Many people have practiced worrying for so long that it has become a mind-set. So my first step is to affirm that habits and mind-sets can be changed.

Next I'll remind myself that worries fall into three categories: 40 percent of worries are about the past; 40 percent of worries are about the future; 20 percent of worries are about the present.

So I'll rid myself of 40 percent of my worries by practicing the art of selective forgetting; I ask myself to stop looking back and worrying about what might have been.

I'll eliminate another 40 percent of my worries by affirming my faith in the future. I remind myself that despite all the troubles and difficulties that may lie ahead, I, with God's guidance, have the ability to respond.

With 80 percent of my worries now eliminated, I make a conscious decision to live in the present moment. I keep my focus on what is left, not what is lost; what is right, not what is wrong; what is good in the circumstances, not what is bad.

Then I'll empty my mind—of anxiety, fear, and insecurity. I'll imagine actually picking up those portions of my thoughts and removing them from my mind.

Finally, I'll fill my mind with peace, courage, calm, and assurance. I imagine putting those elements into my thinking along with a recognition that as long as God is with me, I have no need to worry.

THE DESIRE FOR A PASSIONATE LIFE

I believe passion is the single most powerful unharnessed emotion in the world today. But we tend to have an inaccurate view of what makes for effective passion on a day-to-day basis.

The world tends to look for happiness in huge and dramatic packages. But real joy comes when we shift our awareness to the small and more precious gifts. If we will just become aware of these everyday wonders, it then becomes our privilege to make the most of them. For in fact, the big packages of joy and passion are few and far between. Instead, we need to become aware of life as it is, here and now.

Several years ago I spent the weekend as the guest of the owner of a winery in Australia. He seemed always to be singing and whistling and was full of happiness and good humor, even though he had been diagnosed with cancer. As we sat on his veranda savoring some of his work, I asked him the secret of his happiness. He replied, "Greg, it is a habit of mine to focus on the little things. Just look at this beautiful view," he said, making an expansive gesture with his arm. "It's breathtaking. And every morning when I awaken and every night before I go to sleep, I actually bless my family, the vineyards, the people who work here, and I thank God for the wonderful harvest.

"It was the year before I was diagnosed with cancer, when I was having so many problems, that I realized I had forgotten the happiness habit. I think that was part of the reason I became sick. But I've rediscovered it. And I believe that is part of the reason I'm doing so well."

I have also found the opposite is true. In my research work with senior citizens, studying what makes for longevity, I came to know a woman in Pennsylvania who had arthritis for many years. She was fond of saying, "My arthritis is bad today. I can't do anything. It makes my life miserable."

Every time anyone would talk to this lady, she would drag out the sordid details of her affliction. This dear elderly lady got a lot of attention from her son, her daughter, and the personal care aides. It was her arthritis that seemed to be her magnet. I believe, in a real sense, she enjoyed her

*Cultivating
our passion
takes desire
and a
decision.*

"misery," as she called it. It offered her a way of being in control and of trying to manipulate people into doing things for her.

Passion has two edges. I believe this woman really did not want to be happy.

To be happy we must understand one important point clearly: we must sincerely desire to be happy. Cultivating our passion takes desire and a decision.

To allow the passion that is already ours to come bubbling forth, we need to have an intense desire to carry on a love affair with this experience called life. To know joy we must embrace life, drawing it close to us and sensing the beauty, the wonder, and the goodness in the world.

FORGOTTEN JOY

I often tell our wellness support group participants to get into the habit of laughing. Far too many people have forgotten how to laugh. I see people go through the day with a frown on their face. The corners of the mouth are turned down, the forehead is wrinkled, the eyebrows are pinched together. So many people walk around this way that it is accepted as being natural.

At a recent Texas event, I challenged the group to give me a big toothy grin, a smile so big that the molars would show. Even though I pressed for all the group to do it, only about 10 percent of the participants did. And even though we held that toothy grin for only ten seconds, one woman summed up the experience for most of the others when she said, "If I walked around with that grin on my face, people would think I'm crazy."

She probably spoke the truth. Too bad. We were made to be joyful, we were given the right to be happy. Do you remember how happy a baby can be? A baby will crawl on the floor, pick up toys, perhaps drop the toys, and then gurgle delightedly. When the baby laughs, her or his mouth will open wide in an expression of sheer uninhibited joy. Often there's a scream of delight. There's nothing halfhearted about the joy of a baby.

When a baby looks up at the face of its mother, that baby's face is a beautiful expression of joy. If the mother will respond to the baby's good nature, she, too, will allow herself a few moments of sheer, uninhibited joy. That's passion.

As adults, we tend to forget that we have this ability to experience wholehearted passion. Our needs are more complicated than a baby's. We do need to learn how to be patient and even how to compromise. A grown-up's life is more demanding and at times more frustrating than that of a baby's.

Still, the capacity to let joy bubble out into the world is built into us. If we'll just allow ourselves, we can feel that passion, we can cultivate happiness. Let it come out. Share it with others. Give it a spirit and completeness that will make that joy and passion last and carry over into the rest of our lives.

"Most of the time," said Harold, a retired schoolteacher, "I just don't feel like laughing. Most of the time, I feel like crying."

This attitude runs deeper and is far more pervasive than most people care to admit. We need to allow ourselves to take a good hard look at our own abilities to allow positive passion into our lives. We have them. They may be hidden, it is true, but it is our job to uncover them and show them to the world so that we can feel pride in ourselves and laugh once again. We need to let joy and passion out.

Many people long to live passionate lives, to be driven by an all-consuming desire to carry out their mission. But the word *passion,* to others, stands for the abandonment of "reason" in the reckless pursuit of pleasure. These people might think that running off with an Argentine polo-playing paramour would be the ultimate in passion. But the joy such passion provides is short-lived.

True passion and joy can be found in deeper, subtler moments, in the quiet and deeply committed thoughts and actions of daily living. We find it while carrying out our mission in nursing a baby, making a sales call, or preparing a special meal. Passion motivates us to care for a loved one who is ill, to remember a friend's birthday, or to give of ourselves to a cause.

Every day offers another opportunity to live passionate lives filled with joy rather than passive lives filled with despair. Our task is to remember to say "yes" to life and allow the feelings of joy to bubble through.

It is interesting that both the Koran, the sacred book of Islam, and the Jewish Talmud teach that we will be called to account for every permissible pleasure life offered us that we refused to enjoy.

I know. Like overcoming worry, maintaining joy is a personal struggle for me. I was born to a family in which it was often said, "Now don't have too much fun." I'm not certain what my parents wanted to communicate by that, but at some level I knew it was not OK to laugh with abandon.

Part of that came from a religious upbringing that was twisted. Every Sunday I would be force-marched to the children's classes and then to church. I can remember repeating a responsive reading in which we said, "Man is sinful and unclean." How can you be joyful if that's the lens through which you see the world?

I was also taught that my emotions couldn't be trusted, that they were invariably wrong, and that I needed to keep a tight rein on them every minute. Bad advice.

Emotions can be trusted, particularly the intuitive emotion of joy. True joy is a stellar sign of wellness, one we can follow with certainty. Yes, emotions and intuition need to be tested. They can easily be held up against the master principle of service and the master values of integrity, courage, peace, faith, hope, and love. But once these tests are passed, we can and should follow our intuitive emotions, particularly those of joy and love. And we need to follow them with passion.

"I was so unhappy in my job," said Melanie, speaking of her work as an emergency room X-ray technician. "There's a lot that goes on in an emergency room in a big hospital," she said. "Wonderful cures, but devastating deaths. It took me about six months to realize that what was sticking in my mind were the pain and suffering, not the healing that would result from our efforts. I knew I had to leave or become a cold and unfeeling person just to survive."

Many people in medicine experience this same feeling. They want to help others and still remain warm and caring individuals. To do so requires extraordinary strength and insight. People in the medical community talk about becoming "detached" as a means of protection. But this solution has its price, including diminishing moments of real joy.

For Melanie, a better solution was to redirect her life. "My hospital career was short but useful," she said. "It showed me what I didn't want. Finally I had the nerve to follow my passion. Today, I own two of these Deck the Halls picture and frame shops. And we hope to open a third this coming year. I'm having a ball."

You could tell she was having fun just by looking at Melanie's face. You could see it in her eyes, hear it in her voice; the very way she walked had a bounce to it. Melanie was one of those people who are "so much sunshine to the square inch."

That's joy! And Melanie let her passion out.

JOY AND MISSION

I believe true joy is found only when we are deeply engaged in our life mission. True joy comes as an expression of our inner music; it's a sharing of our happiness; it's celebrating life, even with simple little rituals.

A man wrote to me after hearing me talk about healing rituals in a radio interview. He told me this story of forgotten rituals: his wife had left him and he was completely depressed. He had lost faith in himself, in other people, in God—he found no joy in living.

One rainy morning this man went to a small neighborhood restaurant for breakfast. Although several people were at the diner, no one was speaking to anyone else. Our miserable friend hunched over the counter stirring his coffee with a spoon.

In one of the small booths along the window was a young mother with a little girl. They had just been served their food when the little girl broke the sad silence by almost shouting, "Momma, why don't we say our prayers here?"

The waitress who had just served their breakfast turned around and said, "Sure, honey, we pray here. Will you say the prayer for us?" And she turned and looked at the rest of the people in the restaurant and said, "Bow your heads."

Surprisingly, one by one, the heads went down. The little girl then bowed her head, folded her hands, and said:

> God is great, God is good,
> And we thank him for our food.
> Amen.

That ritual changed the entire atmosphere in this little restaurant. Our friend began to talk to a fellow a few stools down from him. The waitress said, "We should do that every morning." Another customer started talking with the young mother.

"All of a sudden," said our friend, "my whole frame of mind started to improve. From that little girl's example, I started to thank God for all that I did have and stop majoring in all that I didn't have. I started to choose happiness."

It's possible to let joy bubble forth in our lives. We can overcome self-pity, worry, and discouragement. We can change, no matter what our age, no matter what the circumstances. How? I put these steps into action and they help me every time:

The doorway to joy is marked "gratitude." I give thanks for the good things that I have. Some things may look bad, but undoubtedly thousands of things are good. When I focus on the good things, I immediately start acquiring a new outlook.

The doorway
to joy
is marked
"gratitude."

Then I'll find some words of affirmation about the joy in my life, and I repeat them often. Try repeating this phrase every five minutes for a day and see if it doesn't change your life: "My life is filled with glad tidings and great joy."

When things go wrong, I don't go with them. I do my best to let go of the problem. I live the solution. What does this mean? Here are some examples:

Often, I'll find joy by doing something new and different. Perhaps we'll go somewhere or do something that can give us a new perspective. I don't bring the problem with me; instead I seek a fresh and joyful point of view.

Sometimes I share my burden with someone I trust. A friend can help us in many unexpected ways. I feel as if I can be particularly open with my friend Mark, who lives in Michigan. We don't see each other often, but when I need to talk, he's there to listen.

Finally, I'll release my difficulties to God. In my own way, I pray and release. And I always end my prayers by thanking God for all the blessings I do have.

The result is inevitable: if I sincerely approach this exercise just as I have described, joy will bubble forth. I feel a sense of passion return.

I did my best to put joy into practice in my own recovery from almost certain death. After the success of my first book, *The Cancer Conqueror,* I received some exceedingly harsh criticism in the press from a "cult watchdog group." In fact, their threat of picketing forced a church to cancel sponsorship of one of my seminars.

I was devastated. There was no joy in this work. I clearly recall getting on the phone with my friend, Dr. Robert H. Schuller. When I told him what had taken place, his first comment was "Here's your lesson: the dog keeps howling, but the moon keeps shining!"

I was silent. He was silent. I could tell he was gauging my response. But I didn't get it.

Finally, I said, "What in the world are you trying to tell me?"

Dr. Schuller then related this story. "There was a politician who did the best job he could. But being quite human, he made mistakes and was criticized, and reporters repeated errors of fact about him in the newspaper. Our politician friend became so upset that he drove out into the country to visit his dear friend, a dairy farmer. 'What am I going to do?' the politician cried. 'I tried so hard. Nobody has tried harder than I have to do more good for more people—and look how they criticize me!'

"But the old farmer could hardly hear the complaint of his persecuted politician friend because his hound dog was barking at the full moon. The farmer tried to rebuke his dog, but the dog just kept barking.

"Finally, the farmer said to his politician friend, 'You want to know how you should handle your unfair critics? Here's how,' the farmer said as he pointed to the dog. 'Listen to that old dog. Now, look up at that moon. And remember this—people will keep yelling at you, they'll nip at your heels, they'll criticize you. But here's the lesson,' said the farmer as he pointed first to the dog and then to the moon, 'the dog keeps howling, but the moon keeps shining.'

"Let people persecute you," said Dr. Schuller, "but don't stop doing all the good you've been doing. People will try to snatch away your happiness—but don't let them take away the joy that's in your heart."

PASSION AND PERSONAL GROWTH

That is the power of passion. It's turning an adversary into an ally. It's turning an enemy into a friend.

We named our outreach to cancer patients and their families *Cancer Conquerors* in order to express this very idea. What does it mean? The name came from the Bible, the Book of Romans: "We are more than conquerors through him who loved us."

What could top being a conqueror? What is better than winning? It's converting an adversary into an ally. It's taking the message of cancer or any adversity and using it to find passion and personal spiritual growth in our life.

In fact, our troubles can turn into joy almost immediately when we understand them as opportunities for personal spiritual growth. The life lessons are in the message behind the troubles; our troubles actually represent a chance to learn about living. Our job is simply to recognize these opportunities and learn from the messages.

Once we reframe a problem as an opportunity for personal spiritual growth and begin to act on this new perspective, no matter what situation we find ourselves in, we will feel an immediate rush of joy at the core of our being. Our passion returns.

Joy and passion are truly a part of our nature, built into us. They simply need to be let loose in order to heal and harmonize our lives. True joy is completely independent of what our external circumstances may be.

I love the advice of a wise older friend. He was sharing a lesson that he had learned early in his growing up. He had an uncle who was successful in every way. His uncle told him, "When you are with negative-minded people, don't let their ideas take hold of you."

"That was good advice," said my friend, "and I've tried to follow it. Negative thoughts truly are deadly. I think they are as negative and contagious and as devastating as the plague."

Passion, too, is contagious. Just as misery loves company, so does happiness. When you are happy, you can spread it everywhere you go. When you are focused on your vision of a life mission devoted to service of others, and when you are a carrier of joy, you give a happy lift to the world. And this very passion will sustain your pursuit of your life mission through every challenge you face.

Cultivate the garden of passion that you have within you. Then give to others from your overflowing abundance of joy. Watch other worries melt away as your joy affirms life's goodness.

Start now. Make a vow to follow the rules listed here.

FIVE RULES FOR PASSIONATE LIVING

1. Get the joyful habit. Happiness is a habit. Put a smile on inside, and make this feeling a part of who you are. Joy starts with a decision, a desire to be happy.
2. Declare war on self-pity and worry. Challenge every negative thought that enters your mind. When you think,

*Passion
sustains
mission.*

"Oh, this is going to be a terrible experience," challenge that thought by saying, "I can make it great!"

3. Strengthen your self-image. Catch a towering vision of yourself. See yourself as you've been in your very best moments, where joy has been unbounded in your life. Visualize the happy times. Imagine that the future will be joyful.

4. Learn how to smile and laugh. Adults mostly grin and sometimes chuckle. But not many allow themselves really to laugh—I mean a genuine "belly laugh" that gives you a sense of relief and freedom. Relearn to do something none of us should have ever forgotten—to laugh like a child.

5. Help others. Joy in service, serve in joy. The two are so closely intertwined they cannot be accurately separated. Give to your fellow human beings. This will be the most rewarding experience of your life. Joy will inevitably follow. Give for the joy of giving, not for the thought of profit. Help others and you'll help yourself.

Guidance for Passionate Living

1. Uncover a theme from your past experiences that will give you insight into where you can find joy.

List the top five positive experiences you've had in your life. Briefly describe what they were and why the experience brought happiness to you. The experiences may have taken place at home, at work, or at school, or during your free time. You may have been alone, or the experience may have involved others. You may have been paid, or you may have given others money. Simply recall those experiences that you truly enjoyed and that made you feel fulfilled.

Experience: *Why this experience was meaningful to me:*

A. _____   _____

_____   _____

_____   _____

B. _____   _____

_____   _____

_____   _____

C. _____   _____

_____   _____

_____   _____

D. _____   _____

_____   _____

_____   _____

E. _____   _____

_____   _____

_____   _____

Examine what you have written and look for an underlying
theme. For example, "My greatest moments of fulfillment
have come with my family." Or "I can point to the deep satisfaction I received from volunteering as one of my most joyful experiences." If one or two themes are clear, write them
in the space that follows.

_____

_____

_____

2. What's important? Suppose you needed to flee your home
because of an impending disaster and could take along only
ten things that you currently have. What would they be?

_____   _____

_____   _____

_____   _____

What do these choices say about where you attach importance and what gives you joy?

_____

_____

_____

3. What will be important to you at the moment of your death? What will it take in the way of accomplishments, possessions, and legacy to allow you to die with the knowledge that you have lived joyfully?

_____

_____

_____

4. What am I most often doing when I become so absorbed that I lose track of time?

_____

_____

_____

5. My conclusions: I find the most joy by

_____

_____

_____

4

MISSION

Strong reasons make strong actions.

Shakespeare

■ ■ ■

VISION + SERVICE × PASSION = *MISSION*

▪ ▪ ▪

How then should we live?

What Tolstoy said about families—that "all happy families resemble each other while each unhappy family is unhappy in its own way"—turns out to also be true about people with a sense of mission.

People who are living out their life mission resemble each other. They all have the ability to translate vision into reality through service and sustain it with passion. And they are all able to arouse a sense of excitement about the significance of their mission and their contribution to the world.

Norman Cousins told of visiting the great cellist, Pablo Casals. "It was his excitement for his mission that sustained him," said Cousins.

He told the story of his first morning as Casals's houseguest. When the great musician first got out of bed, he was bent over and looked like he was in pain. This was the arthritis that had begun to set in and limit his activities.

After a light breakfast, Casals turned to the cello. "As he did," shared Cousins, "his entire demeanor changed."

His very posture improved. He rubbed his gnarled hands and soon was able to flex his fingers. He stood more upright. A smile came to his face. His eyes grew wider and brighter.

As he picked up the instrument, he rubbed it tenderly, communicating with it and drawing power from the possibilities it represented. This seemed to infuse Casals with even more energy. In a matter of ten minutes, he transformed himself from a person with physical limits to the great cellist that he really was. "This," said Cousins, "was another recognition of the power of the mind-body connection."

This is also the recognition of the transformative power of mission. Those people who become immersed in their mission, who allow their mission to suffuse their thoughts, words, and deeds, are changed people. Missions shape and elevate the motives and goals of these people. A mission achieves its own significance as it unleashes energy in our pursuit of its achievement.

A symbiotic relationship is established between the mission and the missionary. "My writing," said R. L. Stein, the best-selling writer of children's books, "is accomplished by a person unto itself. There is a constant interplay between me and the wordsmith."

A transformative mission is morally purposeful. The missions to which people respond are based on purposes and visions that are linked to the master values they hold dear. The mission itself creates a higher level of moral authority.

Martin Luther King Jr.'s mission was based on the moral imperative that all people are created equal. Mohandas Gandhi's mission set before him the higher values of peace, selflessness, and nonresistance.

Carry a
vision of mission
and
you become a
changed person.

The great Chinese sage Confucius helped a nation recognize that nobility of character is more important than nobility of birth. Mother Teresa's example of helping others brings new definition of service to a needy and hungry world.

Your mission sets standards for your actions. A sense of mission has the potential to move everyone who becomes immersed in it to a higher standard of behavior. The father who takes a stand and says, "As a parent, I cannot condone your use of drugs or alcohol," sets a higher standard for his children as he fulfills his mission of parenting. Sales representatives who vow never to criticize their competition in the pursuit of success raise the level of integrity with which they live out their mission.

Mission elevates; it raises consciousness. Mission generates within the missionary a deep sense of meaning in his or her work and life. Carry a vision of mission and you become a changed person.

MYTHS OF MISSION

All the sparkling promises of having a sense of mission are often dulled by the myths that exist about it. There are a handful that need to be dispelled.

Myth 1

Mission is for the rare individual.

Nothing could be further from the truth.

While the life that is lived as a mission may seem relatively rare, there are literally millions of people fulfilling their mission every day, and many are accomplishing great feats.

Mission is for everyone. It is important to understand that people may be pursuing a mission in one area of their life and have quite an ordinary role in another. I recently spoke at a New Jersey church where the minister was a factory worker. A local auto mechanic was formerly head of a youth organization for the entire Commonwealth of Pennsylvania. A schoolteacher started a volunteer agency that serves over 150,000 people annually. And a housewife whose daughter lost her life to a drunk driver started one of the largest anti-drug, anti-alcohol crusades in the world.

The truth is that people with missions are plentiful. And a mission of importance is within the reach of virtually every person.

Myth 2

You are born with a mission, you cannot make it happen.

Some religions teach that we are preordained to serve certain roles in life. In fact, some teach the doctrine of predestination, which holds that only an elect few will know glory while the rest of us will remain in some state of limbo.

Don't believe it.

The truth is that the ability to implement a mission can be learned. We are nearly all educable, as long as the basic desire to pursue a mission is present.

But even those with impairments have a mission.

A woman plagued by a life of drug and alcohol abuse gave birth to a mentally retarded child. The family encouraged her to "put him in a home" and get on with her life.

"I couldn't do it," she said. "That baby's purpose was to give me a reason to live." Today this mother has been clean and sober for eight years and has started a program that serves parents with children who are developmentally disabled.

Furthermore, the natural endowments we bring to our mission can be enhanced; nurture is far more important than nature in determining the success of a mission.

This does not mean that there is some simple formula, a one-size-fits-all suit of mission clothing that we can slip into. Indeed, the formula offered in this book, Vision + Service × Passion = Mission, requires every person to define each component of the equation for himself or herself.

But do use the formula. Treat it with respect. It contains great truth. The exercise of defining these elements for yourself becomes a deeply human process, filled with trial and error, victories and defeats, facts and intuition—and it leads to a sense of your own special life mission.

Discovering your mission is like learning any skill—your childhood and adolescence provide you with the basic values; books and more formal schooling can help you understand what's going on. But for those who are ready, most of the learning takes place in the experience itself. Mission can be learned. On-the-job training is standard.

Myth 3

Mission requires a person to be superhuman.

Truth: mission requires us to be super-real. Very few people possess the extraordinary charisma and massive talents that we imagine are needed to fulfill a life mission.

Instead, missions are carried out by people who are "all too human." There are the short and the tall, the articulate and the inarticulate, those dressed for success and those dressed for failure, those with outgoing personalities and those who are painfully shy, those with an aggressive style and those who are passive. No attributes in terms of physique or personality must be superhuman in order for a person to implement a mission.

In fact, the reverse seems to be true. In other words, superhuman status is the result of effectively carrying out a mission, not the other way around. Those who are effective at carrying out a mission are granted a certain amount of status, respect, and even awe by those who observe them. This tends to give them a superhuman aura. Note carefully which came first.

Myth 4

The job of carrying out a mission exists only at the top of an organization.

This is obviously false. Whether the organization is a family, a business, or a government agency, there are multiple opportunities for mission for everyone. In a business organization, there are sometimes thousands of mission slots available. In a family, each member has a mission to carry out.

The need for a sense of mission exists at every level. I am confident that this is happening to a greater extent in our world today than ever before. And there will almost certainly be an exponentially greater number of missionary roles available in the future.

Myth 5

The person who is on a mission must control, direct, prod, and manipulate others.

This is perhaps the most damaging myth of all. Mission involves not so much the exercise of power over others as it does the demonstration of power over oneself. And that power is dedicated to the empowerment of others. Mission does require a vision, one that is internalized. It is often common for that internal vision to be shared with others. And that vision, once shared, becomes an attractive goal that draws people to it.

But one essential characteristic of people with a mission is that they have the capacity to build and develop the confidence and abilities necessary for that mission, first in themselves and then in others. Rather than demanding action, people suffused by a sense of mission lead by pulling rather than pushing, by inspiring rather than ordering, by rewarding progress rather than manipulating, and by enabling people to use their own initiative and experiences rather than constraining or denying the validity of others' experiences and actions.

Once these myths have been dispelled, the question then becomes not one of whether I have a mission but rather one of how I can effectively pursue the mission I do have.

For most people, the puzzle of determining what one's mission in life is takes some time. And that is OK. Finding your mission is not a problem that needs to be solved overnight.

As we've suggested, there's a learning process that's involved, much like riding a bicycle. We actually start with a small tricycle: the three wheels give us stability. Then we go to a two-wheeler, but we add the training wheels to the back; we have advanced, but we still need to be held up. Finally, we raise the training wheels and one day actually take them off. And soon, after a fall or two, we're balancing on two wheels and riding on our own. Each stage has to be mastered in turn before the next can be approached.

THE SPIRITUAL DIMENSION OF MISSION

Like the fledgling bicycle rider, most of us must go through several stages as we find our mission. One insightful lens to look through to examine the stages would be that of the spiritual.

Spiritual does not mean religious. Spirituality focuses its energy on the search undertaken to answer questions about a Supreme Being. It includes forgiveness, gratitude, unconditional love, and personal peace. The focus of religion is on person-made systems that hopefully lead to spirituality. These often include developing doctrines that may help you think properly about God and creeds that may convey the essence of God. Our discussion is definitely not religious; it is spiritual.

There are three spiritual aspects to every life mission. And we must discover each part in turn before we can honestly say, "This is my mission." In a sense we will never fully understand any one of these aspects but will always continue to grow in our perception of them.

In both my own quest for mission and that of many other people, I have observed the following three spiritual aspects.

Sometimes these are discovered sequentially, one after the other; often our understanding shifts from one to the other over and over and in no particular order.

1. *Inner Mission.* Our first task is to seek continual personal spiritual growth. The focus is on becoming the type of person who is prepared to fulfill a mission. We must first *be* somebody before we can *do* our mission.

2. *Shared Mission.* From a spiritual perspective, we are to act in concert with others, in the ways made plain to us, to make this world a better place. Part of our mission, when we share it with others, is in our own way to help bring heaven to earth.

3. *Unique Mission.* God has gifted each of us differently. From a spiritual perspective, we are to make the best use of the gift that we most delight in using, putting it to work for God's purposes in the specific places that bring us the most happiness and peace.

Since you are undoubtedly on your own path of personal growth, know that your journey ultimately leads to a mission of a spiritual nature. It is an exciting revelation that your personal spiritual growth has a purpose that is related to this life, as well as to eternity.

So continue on your path with renewed enthusiasm. In a sense, successful mastery of your inner mission is a precondition for pursuing the other dimensions of mission.

Note that part of our mission is shared with many other people. Simply because it is shared does not mean it is somehow less important. The fact is that we are all given dozens of moments every day when we can demonstrate the spiritual dimension of our mission. We all share in this opportunity.

For instance, do we speed up to shut out a driver trying to change lanes, or do we slow down and let him move over? Do we tell the person on the phone that we're simply too busy to be bothered, or do we respond by taking a moment and asking how we can help her? We have an argument with our mate. Do we respond with a frigid silence toward him, or do we take him in our arms, speak truthfully about our hurt feelings, and assure him of our love?

We share in a mission—in a spiritual quest, really. Seen from the spiritual perspective, it becomes clear which choice we are to make each and every time. And from the standpoint of spiritual maturity, we are required to become masters of both inner mission and shared mission prior to graduating to higher levels of unique mission.

Don't misunderstand. Anyone, whether spiritually inclined or not, can benefit from the practice of all aspects of mission. It's just that those who strive to fulfill their missions with the greatest depth will undoubtedly wish to connect their mission to the God of their understanding. That connection offers the power and synergy for exponential progress.

Spiritually, God has already assigned us a unique mission. God has given us talents and has given us the guidance of our Inner Wisdom as to which talents give us the greatest pleasure. These are usually the talents that cause us to lose all sense of time as we use them.

A woman shared her concerns after a bookstore appearance where I was speaking on the spiritual dimensions of wellness. "You're talking about God's will for my life. I'm afraid of God's will. If there's a mission for me, I'd probably have to end up in the jungles of South America. And I can't even stand to go camping."

My comments went something like this: "Yes, we are talking about God's will. No, God's will is not something to fear but to embrace. And you will not be called for a mission in the wilds of the jungle, or the wilds of the city, for that matter, unless you are specially fit for that work."

Our Inner Wisdom is particularly helpful in analyzing our talents and in using those talents to fulfill the will of God for us. It is reassuring to the person on a spiritual path that our mission has already been revealed; we do not have to struggle to discover it. It can be found in our talents and in our Inner Wisdom; it is not written in the sky.

The three aspects of one's mission come together at an important intersection. This is the place God calls *you*— where your talents meet the world's deep needs. From a spiritual perspective, your mission will undoubtedly be one of love.

It seems to me that the person with a spiritual perspective has a unique advantage for fulfilling his or her mission. Love gives such people constant direction, a true-north compass point toward which they can travel without fail. If we simply ask, "What's the loving thing to do?" the next step in implementing our mission becomes increasingly clear.

A reliance on love does not mean that a mission needs to be some abstract emotional concept. Love translates very pragmatically into a sense of mission and even into

---

*Your mission
will undoubtedly
be one of
love.*

---

mission statements. Here are some actual examples of mission statements that encompass a loving and spiritual dimension:

My mission is to guide people to discover God as a real part of their daily lives.

My mission is to offer the world pure foods in order to nurture people's bodies as part of their personal spiritual growth.

My mission is to show love to others and give encouragement to all, particularly those who are ill.

My mission is to teach music to all whom God brings to me, so they can know the joy of their own song.

My mission is to bring laughter into the world so that life does not seem quite so harsh.

My mission is to help people mourn their losses and disappointments and help them feel closer to God.

My mission is to create beautifully landscaped gardens so that people may experience the pleasure of God's natural beauty.

My mission is to report current events through my newscasts so that people might know more accurately what is happening in God's world and determine where they might make a difference.

The spiritual perspective focuses one's life mission as few other lenses can. When we call forth our highest spiritual understanding in the pursuit of our mission, we are most likely to succeed.

THE DEVELOPMENT OF MISSION CONSCIOUSNESS

Central to knowing and fulfilling our life mission is a permanent change in our consciousness. This change rightly includes our words. One way to change our consciousness is through the use of affirmations that acknowledge and strengthen our alignment with our Inner Wisdom's guidance.

Affirmations are declarations, concise statements that communicate to you and to the world the desire of your Inner Wisdom. Affirmations unlock and direct your personal power. They can change you and the world in which you live.

The power of this practice of speaking our affirmations defies rational, scientific explanation. Yet its efficacy has been consistently demonstrated. Most people, however, do not pay attention to the thoughts and words that emanate from their being. Instead, they are content to let their thinking and feeling and speaking be under the control of outside influences—the morning newspaper, a relative's opinion, or the mood of the moment. This is a sure way to make life an unpredictable struggle and to miss many opportunities for fulfilling one's mission.

On the other hand, every person has the potential to change the entire makeup of his or her life. We can tap into this power through the constant use of affirmations that change our consciousness.

As you go through your day focusing on your mission, bring with you one of these powerful affirmations. Repeat it often, both silently and aloud, as circumstances permit. Live the words; allow them to be translated into actions in your life.

Success

"My vision for mission now controls my body, mind, and spirit. I see clearly. I act quickly. My greatest expectations come to pass, through grace, in a perfect way."

"My greatest and endless good comes to pass now."

"All obstacles vanish from my path. Doors of opportunity open, and I know my life mission."

Health

"I am a spiritual being—my body is perfect, made in God's image."

"The light of creation now streams through my every cell. I give thanks for radiant health."

"I am nourished by my Inner Wisdom. Every cell in my body is filled with this healing wisdom. I give thanks for health and happiness."

Supply

"All that is mine by divine right now reaches me in great avalanches of abundance, through grace, in a perfect way."

"I now draw from the channels of abundance in the universe an immediate and endless supply for the pursuit of my mission. All channels are free. All doors are open."

"I thank God for supernatural abundance. My needs for carrying out my mission are always met with plenty."

Happiness

"My endless good now comes to me, through grace, in countless ways."

"Happy surprises come to me each day. I look with wonder at what is before me."

"I am happy, harmonious, radiant, and detached from the oppression of fear."

Love

"As I give love, I receive love, through grace, in perfect ways."

"I love everyone and everyone loves me. Each person is a golden link in my chain of happiness."

"The love of God, coming through me, now dissolves all discord. As I love, I am loved."

Forgiveness

"I sincerely forgive everyone. Everyone forgives me. The gates to my good now swing open."

"As I forgive, I am free from mistakes and the consequences of mistakes."

"As I forgive, God forgives me. I am free."

Faith

"As I am one with God, I am one with all good."

"It is not me but God at work through me. I have confidence in my Inner Wisdom."

"The Lord is my shepherd, I shall not want."

Guidance

"Inner Wisdom now gives me perfect guidance to make the most of every opportunity."

"I am always under the direct inspiration of my Inner Wisdom. I listen and know exactly what to do."

"Your will, not my will; your way, not my way; your time, not my time."

Divine Direction

"The perfect plan for my life now comes to pass, through grace, in a perfect way."

"My body, mind, and spirit are now molded according to the divine pattern within."

"I now fill the place that no one else can fill. I now do the things that I can do and no one else can do."

Choose an affirmation that fits your mission or your current need. Or write a new affirmation that speaks to your personal mission. Carry it with you and read it several times each day. Watch your words create your life by changing your consciousness.

A FINAL WORD

You have a mission in your life. Believe it, with all your heart and mind. It's absolutely true.

There is a gift that you are to give, a donation that you are to make, that no one else can make. The world needs you to make the gift of your talents and your life. And the world stands ready to reward you. The question is being asked of you, "Will you give? Will you embrace your mission?"

Truly, the world has need of you. You were planned and brought about. You didn't choose whether you would come into this world. And you didn't choose where to come into this world. You came when and where you did because it was your destiny.

You were meant to be born. Even if your birth was considered an accident by your parents, even if your biological parents are unknown to you, you were meant to be here now. The truth is that you have been sent at this time and put in this place to carry out a grand design.

Consider for a moment the implications of this exciting truth. Ask yourself, "Why do I feel I was brought into this world? Why at this time? Given my past experiences and current circumstances, what do I sense is expected of me?"

Ponder these issues deeply. Take this quest for your life mission seriously. Think. Learn. Devote yourself to conducting intensive ongoing research about your mission.

Your life is a wonder. When you were conceived, one of the millions of sperm cells produced by your father over his lifetime entered your mother's womb and united with one of the hundreds of eggs produced by your mother over her lifetime. The result is you. Yes, two other cells may have united and still resulted in the birth of a child. But that child would not have been you.

You do have a place to fill, a special need based on the special you. You are one in a trillion, totally unique in interests and talents. You are a miracle by virtue of your very presence. You are not some accident of biology. You are special. You are here, now, where you are, how you are, given the personality you have, with the unique abilities you possess because this is your moment to contribute to the world.

Life has thrust you center stage. You've been put here with expectations. Your life mission is about your response.

Some people believe that life is just chance, not special at all. Those who believe we are here by some accident must also believe the whole universe is an accident. The earth, perfectly rotating on its axis so that we see a sun that rises each and every morning with precision—an accident? Our planet, orbiting in perfect relationship around the sun, so precise that even a change of one degree for one year would result in all of us burning to a crisp or freezing to death—a matter of luck? Birth, life, the inner harmony that our bodies demonstrate, systems and subsystems all working together to sustain our physical reality—just matters of chance?

That's like saying the dictionary is the result of an explosion under a large pile of letters from the alphabet. The letters just happened to end up as words and those words just happened to define other words in bold type and all the boldface words settled from the explosion on sheets of paper in alphabetical order. Preposterous.

Face it. You have been put here on this planet at this time with your personality and your abilities for a reason. No accident accounts for this miracle. You have been designed. And you have been assigned.

You do have a mission. You are here for an important reason. You are meant for greatness.

It may not be greatness as the world defines greatness. Your great mission may be centered on raising a family, nurturing the lives of those in your sphere of care. To many in the world, this is not a "great" calling. Don't believe it.

Perhaps your reason for being focuses on assisting others who are in great need. Your mission may mean helping the underprivileged or reaching out to the disadvantaged. Certainly this is noble work. But by the world's standards, working in a homeless shelter doesn't qualify for greatness. Don't believe that either.

Maybe your mission is widely recognized. Perhaps you have been given a mission of becoming a world leader, a high-profile ruler, always in the media, who is to exercise power and shape public policy for the betterment of humanity. By the world's standards, this represents greatness. Don't believe that either.

Or perhaps you have been given the mission of becoming a steward of great wealth, of creating even more economic prosperity in this world. And the world calls you great. Certainly don't believe that monetary wealth equates with greatness.

Fame and fortune and power are ephemeral. In and of themselves, they are not great and do not constitute a mission; they are tools for implementing a mission. If they are not seen as tools that allow their owner to implement a mission, then they exist only to satisfy ego.

No matter the wealth or lack of it, no matter the fame or lack of it, no matter the power or lack of it, no matter the public recognition or lack of it, mission is not concerned with the "greatness" of the task you have been given or with whether you are perceived as a "great" person by others.

No. Greatness, the way the world defines it, is not the yardstick for the accomplishment of your mission.

Your success in fulfilling your mission is based squarely on the love, the true unconditional love, that you personally demonstrate in pursuing your vision. You can deem yourself successful in your mission only if you first become a person of love, a spirit devoted to the loving service of others.

Yes, this is mission—the life truly worth living. Mission provides a means of perfect self-expression for each person. It is the place that you—and only you—are to fill, something you are to *be* and *do* that no one else can accomplish in quite the same way.

The promise, the payoff, the benefit? Joy and peace—an emotional and spiritual state of heart and mind, a consciousness, characterized by delight, well-being, and genuine happiness, coupled with the inner strength and harmony that result when we gain freedom from disquieting and oppressive thoughts and emotions. Joy and peace are not only possible, they are the *automatic* result of living life on purpose. True joy, peace, and mission are inextricably linked, seamlessly part of your appointment with destiny.

These extraordinary promises are available to you. You need only determine that you will pursue a life of mission now.

Finally, share this hope with others. Mission is something so deep within each of us that it is etched into our very tissues. Mission is a deeply human theme, awaiting all humanity. Help strike a harmonious chord in the heart of those you love and respect. Share these ideas of mission with them, for this sharing is part of each individual's task.

Living out our own life mission, as wonderful as it is, is not enough. Our mission is not the end of the story—it's actually just the beginning. Once we know our own mission, it must be put to use in the world.

So the finale of the quest for mission is a rebirth. We are transformed and we are here to transform. When we share the message of mission with enough people, we will create a new world order. And nothing will ever be the same again.

You have been given a great call. Now answer. And help others to do the same.

*Share
this hope
with
others.*

Guidance for Mission

1. What are the most significant needs of this world that have been made clear to me? How do my talents match them?

2. Begin work on writing a single-page statement of your life mission. Rework it as needed. Complete a draft within the next thirty days.

The Personal Mission Statement of

_____

My life mission is to _____

_____

_____

_____

_____

_____

_____

_____

_____

_____

_____

_____

Signature_____ Date_____

Appendix A

FINDING YOUR
INNER WISDOM

Most people have been taught to deny, ignore, discount, or distrust their intuitive feelings. Many of us have been told so often that our inner promptings are questionable that we have shut them off completely.

But the fact is we do have an Inner Wisdom that can help us. There is a simple process we can use to tap into this Inner Wisdom, and most people find it easy and helpful once they understand the technique.

As you go through the following exercise, remind yourself that you do have this intuitive Inner Wisdom. Just because you may not feel it or trust it at the moment does not mean it is not there. It is like the force of gravity; it's always there. This exercise will help you learn from it.

Here are some simple steps that will help you contact and cultivate your Inner Wisdom:

1. *Relax.* Find a quiet place, free from distractions, and sit in a comfortable position. If you know a particular relaxation or meditation technique that works for you, use it.

I find it helpful to loosen any tight clothing, particularly neckties or belts. I can relax quickly by taking a deep breath and exhaling slowly and completely. As I do, I allow my shoulders to become loose and relaxed. I also take time to relax the muscles in my face, particularly around my eyes and forehead as well as the jaw. Then I'll simply breath slowly and easily, silently saying to myself the word *Relax.*

2. *Center.* Once you feel completely relaxed, allow your awareness to move into an inner place in the core of your body, perhaps near your heart or solar plexus. The physical place is not as important as the mental and emotional place you are going to. Affirm that this place is deep inside of you and that you have access to it. You can do this with a simple affirmation such as "I am now moving deep within me where I can sense and trust my Inner Wisdom."

3. *Ask.* From this deep inner place, begin to ask questions such as "What direction do I need to take in my life at this time?" Or you might ask, "What do I need to know about this situation?" Often we need wisdom for effectively dealing with other people. You might ask, "What do I need to understand about this relationship at this time?" Or for general guidance, ask these questions: "What do I need to know? Where do I need to go? What do I need to do? For whom? What do I need to say? To whom?"

4. *Listen.* Once you have posed the questions, just let them go. Relax quietly and simply be receptive and open.

Take care to notice the thoughts, feelings, or images that come to you in response to the questions you have asked. If you feel no direction, know that this is fine and just let it go for the moment. Guidance does not necessarily come immediately. It often comes later through a growing awareness or feeling about an issue. Or guidance may come through some seemingly external means—a book you read, a friend who offers advice that strikes a strong chord for you, or any number of alternatives. I know a gentleman who confirmed that he was to donate a kidney to a stranger based on a bumper sticker that said, "Kidney donors save lives." Messages are everywhere if we will simply become aware of them.

5. *Test.* When an idea comes, it is imperative to test it against the standards and values that are clear in your own life. Inner Wisdom can be trusted provided it passes the tests of integrity, hope, and love.

Is this idea/action based on absolute truthfulness? Is both the spirit and letter of integrity honored in this endeavor?

Does this idea appeal to people's hopes rather than their fears? Does this idea/action create an expectation of success rather than motivation by fear of failure?

Can this idea be used to bring more love into the world? Will the actions that implement this idea be a demonstration of unconditional love?

If it meets these criteria, act immediately on the direction. If it does not clearly meet these conditions, ask again.

Continue to test. Pause and notice your feelings about the experience and about the response it generates in others. Follow any further intuitive impulses that meet the test criteria. Evaluate how things work out. When they do not work out for the good of all, ask again and be willing to try something different.

6. *Live.* Complete this exercise and then get up and go about your life. Practice these simple meditations once a day, or at the very least three times a week. I find that the morning hours shortly after awakening are the most creative for me. Others find that the best time is before they go to sleep at night. Find out what works for you and follow it.

If you try these steps as they have been suggested and still don't feel any stronger sense of connection with your Inner Wisdom, here are some further suggestions that may help:

—*Stop.* You're probably trying too hard to make something happen instead of simply allowing it to unfold. Many people think that something amazing is supposed to happen when they get in touch with their Inner Wisdom. That's not true. Just listen more deeply than usual and pay attention to what you hear.

—*Record.* If you feel a lot of inner conflict and confusion and can't distinguish your inner guidance from all your other thoughts and feelings, start making detailed notes. Record which voices you identify inside of you and what their messages are.

For example, if you're attempting to discern guidance on a career change, and you receive a message like "Don't take a chance, this is dangerous," label that as fear. If, on the same subject, you receive guidance that says, "This is a new and exciting opportunity; you can succeed," label that voice as encouraging.

Labeling the many voices that you have is helpful. You'll find you have a conservative voice, a risk-taking voice, a playful child's voice, a mischievous voice, a voice that is loving, a voice that is excited, one that is encouraging, one that is skeptical, and even a voice that may be aloof. Undoubtedly you'll hear voices that sound like those of your parents, your spouse, your boss, or others in your life. Simply record them.

—*Be patient.* Don't get caught up in needing to have an immediate answer. Very few things in life require immediate actions. There's nearly always time for some reflection, even if it is only for a few moments.

Don't look for long-term solutions. Inner Wisdom is best at giving us what we need in the moment. We already have received our long-term guidance in the form of our mission. Often our Inner Wisdom is saying, "Just wait, don't do anything, allow yourself time." When clarity is meant to come, it will.

—*Forgive.* If you feel as if you have been without direction and that your life has been blocked for a long period of time, you probably need to do some of the work of forgiveness. Forgiveness is a hugely powerful emotional healer. If you are finding it difficult or even impossible to contact your intuitive feelings, make a list of people whom you need to forgive. Release them; in doing so, you are actually releasing yourself. Once you have begun in a sincere manner to practice emotional release, you will automatically be more in touch with your intuition.

—*Clarify.* If you are following your inner guidance but do not feel more enlivened and aware, then you are probably continuing to confuse your Inner Wisdom with other emotions or impulses. Clarify. Stay with the process of labeling the voices. Respond to those voices that match your master values. Question, again and again, where the guidance is coming from. You can discern.

Finally, remember that developing the ability to be guided by your Inner Wisdom is a lifelong, ongoing process. Like all things, the process seems to run in cycles. There are times when my own inner guidance comes through loud and clear. At other times, I feel confused and lost, uncertain as to why things are happening as they are and not quite sure what to do about them. Trust those times too. Know that eventually you will come out on the other side with greater awareness.

Inner Wisdom is always there awaiting our discovery. It can be trusted if it is tested. We may lose touch with it or misinterpret it at times. We may even try to push it in order to get quick results. But our Inner Wisdom never abandons us. We are never alone.

Appendix B

LIFE MISSION
APTITUDE ASSESSMENT

This exercise can help you identify one or more of the talents that you have been given. Discovering, or even confirming, your existing gifts can be a thrilling experience that will help you find and better understand your life mission.

Respond to each statement on the Life Mission Aptitude Assessment pages that follow, using the following scale:

3 = Definitely true. "I consistently feel this way."
2 = Usually true. "I feel this way often."
1 = Once in a while. "I feel this way some of the time."
0 = Never. "I don't feel this way at all."

Don't be modest. Answer spontaneously and honestly, according to who you are. Do not answer by pretending to be who you would like to be or how someone else thinks you ought to be. Evaluate yourself openly. Ask yourself how true these statements are of you. What has been your personal experience? To what degree do these statements reflect your personal beliefs, attitudes, and actions?

PART ONE

The Life Mission Aptitude Assessment

Record to what extent each statement is true in your life:

> 3 = definitely true
> 2 = usually true
> 1 = once in a while
> 0 = never

_____   1. I find it enjoyable to organize tasks, events, and people.

_____   2. I like to work with my hands to craft objects.

_____   3. I find it enjoyable and am able to challenge people's perspectives with my creations.

_____   4. I first see the potential in people, not their problems.

_____   5. I communicate points to others with clarity and persuasiveness.

_____   6. I joyfully give liberally to people and projects requiring support.

_____   7. I enjoy working behind the scenes to support the work of others.

_____ 8. I consider my home a place to help people in need.

_____ 9. I am frequently asked for my perspective and advice on a variety of issues.

_____ 10. I am able to motivate other people.

_____ 11. I empathize with people who are hurting and want to help them.

_____ 12. I enjoy simplifying ideas so that others can understand them.

_____ 13. I am thorough and detail-oriented.

_____ 14. I enjoy working with different types of tools.

_____ 15. I am skilled in the arts (drama, music, photography, and so on) and enjoy these efforts.

_____ 16. I like to reassure and strengthen people who are discouraged.

_____ 17. I consistently look for opportunities to build relationships with new people.

_____ 18. I often give of myself or my money to causes that stand for the values I hold dear.

_____ 19. I enjoy seeing that routine but needed tasks are accomplished.

_____ 20. I am the first person to welcome a newcomer to a group.

_____ 21. I have a strong automatic sense of what is the right course of action.

_____ 22. I am able to influence others to achieve a vision.

_____ 23. I gain strength from supporting people who are going through painful life experiences.

_____ 24. I enjoy knowing that my efforts will help others.

_____ 25. I often find simple, practical solutions in the midst of chaos and confusion.

_____ 26. I enjoy making things.

_____ 27. I help people better understand themselves and the world through my artistic expression.

_____ 28. I can often instill hope in others.

_____ 29. I easily communicate my message so that it connects with an individual's wants and needs.

_____ 30. I manage my time and money well and feel satisfaction when giving of both.

_____ 31. I willingly take on a variety of responsibilities that will meet the needs of others.

_____ 32. I find myself drawn to the stranger who needs to get connected to others.

_____ 33. I am committed to lifetime growth as both an intellectual and practical exercise.

_____ 34. I adjust my leadership style to bring out the best in others.

_____ 35. I find it rewarding to help people whom others consider beyond help.

_____ 36. I enjoy helping people understand new ideas.

_____ 37. I can provide direction for the most effective course of action from among several alternatives.

_____ 38. I can visualize how something needs to be constructed before I build it.

_____ 39. I like to find new and fresh ways of communicating.

_____ 40. I can reassure people who need courage for the tasks before them.

_____ 41. I am told that strangers feel comfortable around me.

_____ 42. I happily embrace a moderate and simple lifestyle.

_____ 43. I see significance in doing practical tasks.

_____ 44. I like to create a place where people feel they can be at ease.

_____ 45. I am told by others that I have helped them distinguish between fact and fiction.

_____ 46. I enjoy setting goals and effectively deploy people and resources in order to accomplish them.

_____ 47. I have compassion for people who are hurting.

_____ 48. I approach the study of new ideas and subjects systematically.

_____ 49. I like to help organizations and groups become more efficient.

_____ 50. I take pleasure in giving away my hand-crafted gifts.

_____ 51. I can apply various artistic expressions to communications.

_____ 52. I seem to be able to strengthen people who are having doubts.

_____ 53. I openly share with people what I believe and want them to ask me about my life.

_____ 54. I like knowing that my personal assistance and financial support make a difference in others' lives.

_____ 55. I can spot the small things that need to be done and often do them without being asked.

_____ 56. I enjoy entertaining people and opening my home to others.

_____ 57. I have a deep knowledge about important life-shaping principles.

_____ 58. I seem to influence others to perform to the best of their capability.

_____ 59. I quickly look beyond a person's handicaps and problems and see a life that has a mission.

_____ 60. I am able to communicate in ways that motivate people to want to learn and grow.

_____ 61. I enjoy learning about how organizations best function.

_____ 62. I am good at and enjoy working with my hands.

_____ 63. I am creative and have a vivid imagination.

_____ 64. I like to motivate others toward personal growth.

_____ 65. I openly and confidently tell others about my life and its lessons.

_____ 66. I give generously of my time, my talents, and my financial resources.

_____ 67. I feel comfortable being a helper, assisting others to do their job more effectively.

_____ 68. I do whatever possible to make people feel they belong.

_____ 69. I often find ideas in my reading and studies that I share for the benefit of others.

_____ 70. I am able to shape a vision that others want to be part of.

_____ 71. I enjoy bringing hope and joy to people who are in difficult circumstances.

_____ 72. I like to present information to others in a way that makes it easy to grasp and apply.

_____ 73. I can visualize an approaching event, anticipate problems, and develop alternate plans.

_____ 74. I am good at designing and constructing things

_____ 75. I often need to spend time alone to reflect and develop my creativity.

_____ 76. I am able to challenge others, and they typically respond positively.

_____ 77. I seek out opportunities to talk with others, particularly people I don't know.

_____ 78. I believe I have been given financial abundance so that I might help others.

_____ 79. I happily use my talents and abilities to help wherever needed.

_____ 80. I can make people feel at ease, even in unfamiliar surroundings.

_____ 81. I confidently share my knowledge and insight with others.

_____ 82. I have the ability to determine where we need to go and to help others get there.

_____ 83. I relate to people who are in need and can give practical assistance to help them out.

_____ 84. I enjoy explaining things so that people can grow personally and spiritually.

PART TWO

The Life Mission Aptitude Assessment

Using the grid that follows, transfer your answer to each statement on the Life Mission Aptitude Assessment to the block whose number corresponds to that of the statement. Total the values for each category.

Talent	Response							Total Value
Administration	1	13	25	37	49	61	73	_____
Craftsmanship	2	14	26	38	50	62	74	_____
Artistry	3	15	27	39	51	63	75	_____
Encouragement	4	16	28	40	52	64	76	_____
Communications	5	17	29	41	53	65	77	_____
Charity	6	18	30	42	54	66	78	_____
Helping	7	19	31	43	55	67	79	_____
Hospitality	8	20	32	44	56	68	80	_____
Knowledge	9	21	33	45	57	69	81	_____
Leadership	10	22	34	46	58	70	82	_____
Compassion	11	23	35	47	59	71	83	_____
Teaching	12	24	36	48	60	72	84	_____

By noting which one, two, or three aptitudes listed here end up with the largest total value, you now have some indication of which aptitudes for mission you may have.

My top three aptitudes for mission are:

1. _____

2. _____

3. _____

PART THREE

What Do These Identified Aptitudes Mean?

With this indication of what your top three aptitudes for mission are, you can now go on to determine where these gifts may lead you to serve. Read the sections that follow that describe the aptitude for which you had the highest score.

Then look at the list of vocations and opportunities for service that match these talents. Remember that there are as many ways to serve as there are things to do in this world. Thus a complete listing is impossible.

The Aptitude for Administration

This gift allows you to assume oversight for the efficient execution of an organization's mission. People with this aptitude have the special ability to plan and organize in order to accomplish agreed-upon goals. This talent allows you to organize people, tasks, and events easily. Being adept at delegating responsibilities, financing projects, and solving problems is an indication that you have an aptitude for administration. If your talent lies in this area, then your life mission may be to contribute to an organization's ability to meet the needs of the people it serves.

Serving with this talent: Office managers; program managers; special project management; financial planning and control.

The Aptitude for Craftsmanship

This gift allows those who possess it to enjoy using their hands to meet the tangible needs of other people. The ability to design and build objects is one aspect of this talent. Adeptness at working with tools and raw materials is also part of this talent. Craftsmanship serves as a mission when its product provides a benefit to those who use it.

Serving with this talent: Carpentry; painting; plumbing; electrician; mason; crafts; teaching of these skills.

The Aptitude for Artistry

People with this gift are able to communicate through a variety of art forms. These forms include drama, writing, art, music, dance, and so on. Artistry serves as a mission when its communication captivates people and causes them to consider life from a fresh perspective.

Serving with this talent: actor; writer; fine artist; graphic artist; musician; dancer.

The Aptitude for Encouragement

People with this gift call forth the best from others. This talent serves as a mission as it assists others to become more dedicated, bolsters others when they are discouraged, and challenges others to reach for new goals and higher levels of service.

Serving with this talent: counseling; work with youth; ministry; work with the elderly; prison outreach. This talent is not vocation-specific but can be shared by all.

The Aptitude for Communication

This gift allows the person who possesses it to relate effectively to a wide variety of people on the subject of their expertise. Communicators point out with clarity and conviction, and often with persuasiveness, the rightness of new ideas. They are relationship builders whose life mission may be to call others to new and greater levels of service.

Serving with this talent: sales; ministry; administrator; leader.

The Aptitude for Charity

People with this gift give of themselves and their resources cheerfully and liberally. They commit themselves to the betterment of society and individuals through projects that require them to invest of themselves. They often are able to limit their own lifestyle in order to give as much as possible to others. They also often have a special ability to make money so that it can further their work.

Serving with this talent: financial support of nonprofit organizations; fund-raising chairperson; volunteer.

The Aptitude for Helping

This gift allows people who possess it to accomplish practical and necessary tasks that free up, support, and meet the needs of others. People with this talent for mission serve behind the scenes wherever needed and support the work of others. They are able to attach value to practical service and enjoy knowing that they are releasing others to serve.

Serving with this talent: nurse; organizer of volunteers; assistant in projects; person in charge of meals; person who arranges transportation; secretarial/administrative assistant.

The Aptitude for Hospitality

People with this gift create an environment where other people feel valued and cared for. They meet and welcome new people and create a safe and comfortable setting where relationships can develop. They seek to connect people.

Serving with this talent: This talent is not vocation- or gender-specific. Entertaining at home or in a business environment is a common application of this talent.

The Aptitude for Wisdom

People with this gift possess special insight and understanding that serves others. They are often able to sort out right from wrong, good from bad, best from better, pure motives from mixed motives. They also are often able to point out inconsistencies and appropriately bring them to the attention of those who need to know.

Serving with this talent: board member; doctor; attorney; judge; counselor.

The Aptitude for Leadership

This gift allows its possessor to motivate people to accomplish harmoniously a vision that he or she has set before them. A talent of leadership allows a person to grasp the "big picture" and communicate it to others. People with this aptitude provide direction for organizations, model shared values, set goals, and take responsibility for finding others who will help attain these goals.

Serving with this talent: service on governing boards; key officer in organization; leading community outreach programs; starting a new business.

The Aptitude for Compassion

People with this gift are able to give cheerful and practical service to those who are suffering and in need. This talent allows one to focus on alleviating the sources of pain and suffering, especially for those who may seem least deserving of such help. This talent often leads one to a concern with the individual or social issues that oppress people.

Serving with this talent: health care professional; social worker; comforting the bereaved; ministry.

The Aptitude for Teaching

People with this gift can understand, clearly explain, and motivate others to understand the subjects in which they are interested. These people effectively impart information vocally, visually, and by example. They give time to preparation, study, and reflection. They challenge their student to lifetime learning.

Serving with this talent: teacher; instructor; coach.

These descriptions are just a partial list of talents for missions. If you look carefully, you will see that these talents suggest directions you might take in two of the critical areas of finding your mission: vision—the "Who am I?" question; and service—the "What makes for greatness?" question. Your specific skills will enlarge this list. Experiment. A mission is awaiting your discovery.

MORE ABOUT THE WORK OF
Greg Anderson

Greg Anderson is co-founder and chairman of the American Wellness Project. This effort is devoted to the ongoing development of individuals and organizations based on the concepts of total well-being.

Our vision . . .
is to be people who
collectively put into daily practice
the greatest force in the Universe—
unconditional love.

Our mission . . .
is to empower people and organizations to
enhance their health and enrich their lives through
the understanding and practice
of total wellness.

This process of empowerment is carried out through seminars, workshops, and wellness-based support groups. The American Wellness Project provides on-site wellness development programs for business, healthcare, educational, and government organizations.

For information on these services and guidelines for establishing a local American Wellness Project Group in your area, please contact:

The American Wellness Project
P.O. Box 238
Hershey, PA 17033

1-800-238-6479
www.wellness.net